What Others

"*The Visible Presence* is food for spiritual growth based on newly compiled research about the shadows of Christ in the Bible from start to finish. Every Bible student and teacher will benefit from John's fresh, crisp writing style, exegetical excellence, and personal reflection."

– **Dr. Dearing Garner,** Director of Pastoral Care, *Baptist Child, and Family Services*

"In his book, The Visible Presence: Appearances of Christ in the Old Testament, John Burris sets out to 'put the pieces together' admitting upfront that for him, 'it is a constant battle for my faith to outweigh my logic.' Having thus identified with many of us, Burris presents a well-documented, scripturally based, portrait of Christ in the Old Testament, taking on such challenges as the location of Jesus before Bethlehem, Jesus' place in the Trinity, and Jesus as 'the Angel of the Lord.'

Beginning with Christ's appearance to Abraham, Isaac and Jacob, Burris traces appearances of Christ through the remainder of the Old Testament before offering a very helpful appendix of, 'thirty-nine pre-incarnate appearances Christ in the Old Testament.' This is not light reading, but it is challenging reading. Take your time. Read slowly. Evaluate and enjoy."

– **Dr. Dan Crawford,** Senior Professor of Evangelism & Missions; Chair of Prayer Emeritus, *Southwestern Baptist Theological Seminary*\

"When John Burris became a staff member of the Kingwood First Baptist Church, I had just retired from being a Director of Missions. What struck me when I met him was his insatiable thirst for truth in the Bible. That thirst brought about The Visible Presence. His thorough research and insight on the subject manner, makes this book a must read for preachers, teachers of the Bible and lay leaders.

Many preachers and teachers shy away from discussing this subject because of the extensive research that would be needed to properly present the material. A careful study of this book would give the confidence needed to develop messages, lessons and presentations which would reveal clearly our Lord's actions in the Old Testament. Thank you, John Burris for your dedication and integrity in your research."

– **Dr. Eliu Camacho**, South Central Regional Manager, *My Hope Project*, Billy Graham Evangelistic Association

THE
VISIBLE
PRESENCE

Appearances of Christ
in the Old Testament

John M. Burris

7710-T Cherry Park Dr, Ste 224
Houston, TX 77095
(713) 766-4271

Printed in the United States of America

ISBN: 978-1-0878-0380-7

Acknowledgments

Many people have their fingerprints on this book. A special thanks to my dear friend Ben Lee who used his expertise in journalism and his own professional writing career to make the first attempt at cleaning up the mistakes of a first writing project.

I am also indebted to two wonderful servants of God, Clark and Katelyn Fertitta. Without their help, this book would not be a reality.

To Kingwood First Baptist Church for allowing me a sabbatical to accomplish the bulk of my writing. These last 15 years with you have been a great blessing to my family. I'm looking forward to at least 15 more years serving alongside you.

My wife, Jenny and my children, Jenna and Jackson, thank you for your unwavering support. The three of you are my only earthly treasures.

All glory, honor and praise to Jesus Christ, "This One who is majestic in His apparel, marching in the greatness of His strength, speaking in righteousness, mighty to save." (Isaiah 63:1)

Table of Contents

Preface

I've always been a fan of jigsaw puzzles. There is, apparently, something in me that yearns to put the pieces together. I don't know that it is as much about what the picture of the puzzle looks like. Often, I find, having put in the last piece, that I don't even look at the completed picture. The intriguing aspect for me is completing the puzzle. As you can imagine, a puzzle with a missing piece sends me into quite a "fit."

This mindset also carries over into my understanding of faith and the Bible. Faith, in the Biblical sense of being certain of what I cannot see, does not come particularly easy for me. For me, concepts and ideas are more readily accepted if they "fit together" or make sense logically. And, since the Bible says in Isaiah 55:8, "For My thoughts are not your thoughts, neither are your ways My ways," declares the LORD", my logic is not anywhere near on par with the Almighty. Therefore, it is a constant battle for my faith to outweigh my logic. As a teacher of the Bible, I find myself saying often that we will not be able to "completely understand God." And, while I say it with my lips, my heart still yearns to know Him more fully.

This book is my attempt to meld my faith and my own need for things to "fit together." It is my way of ordering truths of Scripture in a way that brings understanding to my feeble mind. My hope is that you will find, as I have, that there can be great comfort found even in a mystery… the mystery of the One who makes the invisible visible.

John Burris

Kingwood, Texas

of the Trinity."[4] Many theologians refer to the appearances of God in these passages, and others like them, as "theophanies" (Greek: *theos* = "God" + *phaino* = "appear") or "Christophanies." So these words mean "appearances of God" and "appearances of Christ," respectively.[5]

Dr. J. Oliver Buswell writes, "The incarnation differs from all other theophanies in that when He 'was born in Bethlehem.' When He 'became flesh,' He took to Himself, permanently, a genuine human nature, wholly apart from sin. In the Old Testament theophanies He appeared as a man in specific times and places without actually becoming a member of the human race."[6]

To me, this gives whole new meaning to the name Immanuel, God with us. Christ took on human flesh to identify with us.

Where, then, was the Son of God prior to the manger? What was the Son of God doing for all those thousands of years before He was laid in the manger? This is the Glorious Mystery…that Christ has always been the person of the Godhead who reveals God so that man can encounter Him. In other words, the Visible Presence of God.

There are several passages of Scripture that declare that God is unseen and invisible.

---

[4] *Merriam-Webster, s.v.* "pre-incarnate," accessed April 20, 2016, http://www.merriam-webster.com/dictionary/pre-incarnate
[5] Tim Chaffey, "Theophanies in the Old Testament", accessed April 20, 2016, https://answersingenesis.org/jesus-christ/incarnation/theophanies-in-the-old-testament/
[6] James Oliver Buswell, Jr., *A Systematic Theology of the Christian Religion*, 2 vols. (Grand Rapids: Zondervan, 1962), 1:33.

Exodus 33:20

But He said, "You cannot see My face, for no man can see Me and live!"

John 1:18

No one has seen God at any time; the only begotten God who is in the bosom of the Father, He has explained Him.

John 5:37

And the Father who sent Me, He has testified of Me. You have neither heard His voice at any time nor seen His form.

John 6:46

Not that anyone has seen the Father, except the One who is from God; He has seen the Father.

Colossians 1:15

He is the image of the invisible God, the firstborn of all creation.

1 Timothy 1:17

Now to the King eternal, immortal, invisible, the only God, be honor and glory forever and ever. Amen.

1 Timothy 6:15-16

He who is the blessed and only Sovereign, the King of kings and Lord of lords, who alone possesses immortality and dwells in unapproachable light, whom no man has seen or can see. To Him be honor and eternal dominion! Amen.

Hebrews 11:27

By faith he left Egypt, not fearing the wrath of the king; for he endured, as seeing Him who is unseen.

1 John 4:12

No one has seen God at any time; if we love one another, God abides in us, and His love is perfected in us.

However, some of these same Scriptures indicate that even though God (by implication, the Father) is unseen or invisible, the Son, Jesus Christ, has made Him visible.

John 1:14

[14] *And the Word became flesh, and dwelt among us, and we saw His glory, glory as of the only begotten from the Father, full of grace and truth.*

John 1:18

No one has seen God at any time; the only begotten God who is in the bosom of the Father, He has explained Him.

John 14:9

Jesus *said to him, "Have I been so long with you, and yet you have not come to know Me, Philip? He who has seen Me has seen the Father; how can you say, 'Show us the Father'?

2 Corinthians 4:4-6

⁴in whose case the god of this world has blinded the minds of the unbelieving so that they might not see the light of the gospel of the glory of Christ, who is the image of God. ⁵For we do not preach ourselves but Christ Jesus as Lord, and ourselves as your bond-servants for Jesus' sake. ⁶For God, who said, "Light shall shine out of darkness," is the One who has shone in our hearts to give the Light of the knowledge of the glory of God in the face of Christ.

Philippians 2:5-8

⁵Have this attitude in yourselves which was also in Christ Jesus, ⁶who, although He existed in the form of God, did not regard equality with God a thing to be grasped, ⁷but emptied Himself, taking the form of a bond-servant, and being made in the likeness of men. ⁸Being found in appearance as a man, He humbled Himself by becoming obedient to the point of death, even death on a cross.

Colossians 1:15

15 He is the image of the invisible God, the firstborn of all creation.

The word "image" in this verse is the Greek word *eikon*. It means a precise copy or reproduction. This word is the origin of our English word, icon.

John Macarthur writes, "All that God is essentially is in Christ. He is the very essential nature of God as well as manifesting the very communicable attributes of God. Theologians would say He is the incommunicable God as to His essence and He manifests the communicable attributes of that incommunicable essence. He is what God is and He manifests what God is to all those who see Him. To see Him is to see God."[7]

Colossians 2:9

9 For in Him all the fullness of Deity dwells in bodily form,

Hebrews 1:3

3 And He is the radiance of His glory and the exact representation of His nature, and upholds all things by the word of His power. When He had made purification of sins, He sat down at the right hand of the Majesty on high,

Here, the author of Hebrews refers to Christ as the exact representation of God's nature. The Greek word for exact representation is the word *charakter*. This is the only time in the New Testament this word is used. According to the New Testament NAS Greek Lexicon, the word means...

- *the instrument used for engraving or carving*

- *the mark stamped upon that instrument or wrought out on it*

- *a mark or figure burned in (Lev. 13)*

- *stamped on, an impression*

---

[7] John MacArthur, "The Nature of the Incarnation, Part 2" www.gty.org Accessed June 29, 2016.
http://www.gty.org/resources/sermons/80-207/the-nature-of-the-incarnation-part-2

- *the exact expression (the image) of any person or thing, marked likeness, precise reproduction in every respect, i.e. facsimile[8]*

---

[8] The NAS New Testament Greek Lexicon. "Charakter" www.biblestudytools.com Accessed June 29, 2016. http://www.biblestudytools.com/lexicons/greek/nas/charakter.html

Chapter Two

A Name Above All Names

"There are two hundred and fifty-six names given in the Bible for the Lord Jesus Christ, and I suppose this was because He was infinitely beyond all that any one name could express."

- Billy Sunday

So, I have to be honest. I did trick you a bit with that opening sentence of the first chapter. Notice that I didn't say "Jesus" did not originate from the womb of Mary. I used the name "Christ." If you've read much of the Bible, you will know that many names are used to refer to the Son of God. Which one is correct? Well, all of them. But, it is important to know which name means what.

The name Jesus was a common name among first century Jews. Jesus is the Greek rendering of the Hebrew name Joshua. Seen in this light, we see that the name appears to be rather common. Speaking of the child born to Mary, the angel said, "She will bear a Son; and you shall call His name Jesus, for He will save His people from their sins."[9] The name Jesus should be more familiar to us than we think. It is equivalent to the Hebrew name Joshua.

---

[9] Matt. 1:21 NASB.

The Greek meaning of Jesus is "Jehovah is my help," or, "Jehovah is rescue."[10] William Barclay notes, "The very name stamps Jesus as Saviour. He is God's divinely appointed and divinely sent Rescuer, whose function it is to deliver men from their sins."[11]

But, if Jesus were the common name, the designation "Christ" was so uncommon that it was wrought with a great deal of controversy. Christ was more of a title than a name. It would have been more typical for first century Jews to refer to Jesus as, "Jesus, Son of Joseph" or "Yehoshua ben Yosef."[12] The title, "Christ", comes from the Greek word for Messiah, which means "anointed one."[13] It was this title that set Jesus of Nazareth apart from everyone else.

It must be understood, however, that the Jewish thought of Messiah may not have been what we might think. This may explain why many Jews may have missed Him. In fact, it is difficult to find a direct reference to "The Messiah" in the Old Testament. The most direct reference is in the book of Daniel, "Then after the sixty-two weeks the Messiah will be cut off and have nothing, and the people of the prince who is to come will destroy the city and the sanctuary..."[14]

---

[10] William Barclay, "Jesus as They Saw Him", in *The Book of Jesus* ed. Calvin Miller (New York: Simon and Schuster, 1996), 37.

[11] Barclay, 37.

[12] J.D. Stone, "Jesus' Name", accessed March 31, 2016, http://jdstone.org/cr/files/jesusname.html (2009)

[13] The Revell Bible Dictionary, "Jesus" (New Jersey: Fleming H. Revell Company, 1990), 556.

[14] Daniel 9:26 NASB

According to Walter Kaiser, "The Hebrew term, *masiah*, appears thrity-nine times in the OT and is rendered in the Septuagint by the Greek *christos*, which became the official designation for Jesus in the NT and, at first, a pejorative way of referring to his followers: 'Christians'."[15] Certainly the word "messiah" is found in other places, but it is found being applied to people (most notably, prophets, priests and kings...Lev. 4:5, 6:22, Isaiah 61:1, 1 Sam. 10:1, 16:13), objects such as the altar or armor and even to the nation of Israel. (Num. 7:10, Isaiah 21:5) The word itself is a transliteration of a Hebrew word. The word means "anointed thing" or "anointed one." Always the word is applied to a person or thing that has been set aside for service to God.

Robert L. Cate notes, "But the term, messiah, was ultimately applied to the ideal Davidic ruler of the future."[16] The nation of Israel did not have a glorious past to look back to after the Garden of Eden. It seemed to be one struggle and disappointment after another. The life of Moses and the deliverance from Egyptian bondage did provide a spiritual marker of God's favor, but the subsequent wandering of the children of Israel further drove home the fact that all was not right in the nation.

Soon the Israelites cried out for a King who would make them as prosperous as other nations. (1 Samuel 8-12) That would prove to be disastrous as well. Not until David did there come a hope for Israel. But, as we know, David had his struggles as well.

---

[15] Walter C. Kaiser, *The Messiah in the Old Testament* (Grand Rapids: Zondervan Publishing House, 1995), 15.
[16] Robert L. Cate, *Old Testament Roots for New Testament Faith* (Nashville: Broadman Press, 1982), 213.

Again, Robert L. Cate offers great insight. "Aside from his personal, human failures, however, there was an assurance that God had chosen him for a special service. Further, God had used David to bring about the only truly great achievements in Israel's national history. Further, to David had been promised future blessings for his family and, through them, to his people."[17]

This idea led to an expectation that each king in David's line could be that "messiah." As you may know, the descendants of David were a rollercoaster of faithful and wicked. There never seemed to be any consistency. Add to this the fact that neighboring nations seemed to have powerful rulers and great success. Please understand that God had in mind a Redeemer, a Savior from before the foundation of the world that would restore God's people to a relationship with Him. Unfortunately, Israel did not fully comprehend that notion. (Jeremiah 23:5)

As Robert Cate says of the concept of kingship in the Old Testament, "The royal ideology of the ancient Near East may have played some part here. In the nations which were Israel's neighbors, the king was seen as being the god's representative, the god's son, and sometimes was even identified with the god. Certainly, Israel looked for some things from the future Messiah of God that the surrounding nations claimed for their reigning kings."[18]

In other words, they developed a concept of a future ideal ruler who would be God's ideal representative for His people. In doing

---

[17] Cate, 213.
[18] Cate, 214.

Chapter Three

God in Three Persons

"Bring me a worm that can comprehend a man, and then I will show you a man that can comprehend the Triune God."

- John Wesley

The Doctrine of the Trinity is perhaps the most difficult doctrine of the church. To even begin to try and get complete understanding, one only becomes more frustrated that our minds are incapable of grasping the reality of its concepts.

Jonathan Edwards noted, after studying the topic extensively, "I think [the doctrine of the Trinity] to be the highest and deepest of all Divine mysteries."[24] I would not pretend to have unraveled this great mystery, but we can, at least, consider the basic structure of the doctrine.

Matt Perman has written, "The doctrine of the Trinity means that there is one God who eternally exists as three distinct Persons--the Father, Son, and Holy Spirit. God is one in essence and three in person. These definitions express three crucial truths: (1) The

---

[24] Oliver Crisp, *Jonathan Edwards on God and Creation* (Oxford: Oxford University Press, 2012), 119.

Father, Son, and Holy Spirit are distinct Persons, (2) each Person is fully God, (3) there is only one God."[25]

Now, that we all completely understand the Trinity, we can move on, right? No? First of all, understand that the word trinity is not a Biblical word. You will not be able to look up the word trinity in your concordance and go to a verse for confirmation. It is a doctrine expressed through the overall teaching of God's Word. Second, understand that there is not an illustration or word picture or a concept that we are familiar with that will adequately express the idea of the trinity. As Wayne Grudem says, "all analogies have shortcomings."[26]

The best way to gain a basic understanding, although one that must be accepted by faith, is to take each of the three premises of the definition and cite Scripture to affirm each one.

1) **God is Three Persons**- Gen. 1:26, Gen. 3:22, Gen. 11:7, Isaiah 6:8, Isaiah 48:16, John 14:26, John 15:26, John 17:24. The Hebrew word for God is *Elohim* which, in the language, is plural.

2) **Each person is Fully God**- Gen. 1:1, Matt. 28:19, John 1:1, Eph. 4:4-6, Col. 2:9, Heb. 1:3

3) **There is Only One God**- Deut. 6:4, Isaiah 45:5-6, 1 Tim. 2:5

[25] Matt Perman. "What is the Doctrine of The Trinity?" www.desiringgod.org January 23, 2006. Accessed March 31, 2016. http://www.desiringgod.org/articles/what-is-the-doctrine-of-the-trinity
[26] Wayne Grudem, *Systematic Theology* (Grand Rapids: Zondervan, 1994), 240.

Grudem says, "Each person of the Trinity has all the attributes of God, and no one person has any attributes that are not possessed by the others. The only way it seems possible to do this is to say that the distinction between the persons is not a difference in 'being' but a difference in 'relationships'. The only difference between them is the way they relate to each other and to the creation."[27]

This picture, called The Shield of The Trinity, illustrates this idea…

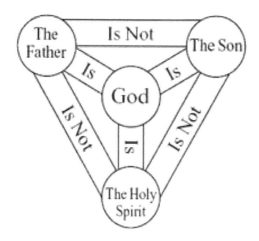

Even though the Bible does not directly affirm the Trinity, as if Paul or John would write, "Now, let me explain to you the Trinity," there is evidence of the triune nature of God in the text of Scripture.

For example, in the very first line of the Bible, a word is used to imply the Trinity. "In the beginning God created the heavens and the earth."[28] The Hebrew word for God in that verse is *Elohim*. The "im" ending on a Hebrew word implies a plural. That Hebrew

---

[27] Grudem, 253-254.
[28] Gen. 1:1 NASB

word is also used in the Shema which says that "Hear, O Israel! The Lord is our God, the Lord is one!"[29] So, God, *Elohim* (plural) is **one**.

There are also passages that use plural pronouns in speaking of God's activity.

- "Let **Us** make man in **Our** image; according to **Our** likeness"- Genesis 1:26

- "Behold, the man has become like one of **Us**, knowing good and evil…"- Genesis 3:22

- "Come, let **Us** go down and there confuse their language…" – Genesis 11:7

- "Whom shall I send, and who will go for **Us**?" – Isaiah 6:8

Ervin Hershberger presents two interesting lines of thought regarding the validity of the Triune nature of God. First, he notes that God created the Universe with many triads and trinities.[30] He goes on to list six examples.

A. The universe is a trinity of time, space, and matter. Each of these fills everything, everywhere, all the time.

B. Time is a trinity of future, present, and past. The present always flows out of the future, and moves on into the past.

C. Space has length, breadth, and height (or depth). All are everywhere all the time— never missing any place.

---

[29] Deut. 6:4 NASB
[30] Ervin N. Hershberger, *Seeing Christ in the Old Testament* (Harrisonburg: Vision Publishers, 2010), 16.

D. Matter exists as energy, motion, and phenomena. All are omnipresent; and motion coming out of energy produces phenomena (experienced by physical senses).

E. The sun is light, heat, and energy. "There is nothing hid from the heat thereof" (Psalm 19: 6).

F. Man consists of spirit, soul, and body. He is made in the image and likeness of the holy Trinity (Genesis 1: 26).[31]

Secondly, Hershberger points out that God's most basic attribute of His character is love. He writes, "We all agree that 'God is love' (1 John 4:8,16). Love requires relationship, and without plurality there is no relationship. Therefore, it is self-evident that even when there was nothing but GOD- before creation began- God was a plurality, for 'God is love.'"[32]

Let me give you two reasons why I believe we cannot fully explain the Doctrine of the Trinity.

1) To maintain the mystery and majesty and "one of a kind" nature of God, He cannot be fully comprehended. If we can explain God, He must not be God.

2) Because of the natural tendencies of man to "explain" God, or rationally understand Him, he kept His people from falling into the error of humanity that is a multiplicity of gods.

---

[31] Hershberger, 16.
[32] Hershberger, 17.

For our study, it is only necessary for us to have an understanding that:

1) Christ is God

2) Christ is eternal

Why should we try to understand a mystery that no one apart from God can fully explain? By understanding that Christ is Divine and therefore has always existed and exists for all eternity sets the stage for us to look for Him on the pages of the Old Testament.

Chapter Four

The Logos

In the beginning was the Word, and the Word was with God, and the Word was God.

– John 1:1

This passage presents a strange word that describes Christ. The Greek word for "Word" in the passage is *Logos*.

Simply put, Logos means the full expression. It was a word that fundamentally meant to speak or the spoken word. But, it had a specific background in Greek culture.

R.C. Sproul states, "Ancient Greek philosophy was concerned with answering the ultimate questions of reality. They wanted to find the ultimate reality that lies behind all things."[33]

Eventually, they came up with a term that would describe this ultimate reality. That term was Logos. It came to mean that which gave life and meaning to all that existed. But, given their lack of belief in the one true and living God, this Logos became known as some kind of impersonal force.

---

[33] R.C. Sproul, "Logos" www.ligonier.org Accessed April 19, 2016. http://www.ligonier.org/learn/devotionals/logos

In fact, Greek philosophers believed this "creative force" to be present at the very beginning of creation. "This idea of a 'creative force' present in the act of creation came, originally, from the Greek philosopher Heraclitus, who lived in Ephesus about 500-years before the birth of Jesus. Incidentally, church tradition holds that John the Apostle spent the latter part of his ministry in Ephesus where this philosophical notion would have been commonly known. Heraclitus used the term to indicate the principle of order that made all the difference at creation between chaos, which was always there, and the ordered universe as we know it. Heraclitus decreed, "all things come to pass in accordance with this logos."[34]

Jewish Philosophers had a similar concept of the "Logos." "Philo of Alexandria, a Greek-speaking Jew, who was a contemporary of Jesus of Nazareth, had adopted the term logos in Jewish philosophy to mean 'an intermediary divine being' or 'demiurge'. He tried to explain why the world created by the one true and perfect God isn't perfect. Philo followed the Platonic distinction between perfect ideas and imperfect matter, which needed intermediary beings to bridge the gap. In his philosophy, the logos was the highest of these intermediary beings. Philo even went as far as calling the logos "the first-born of God." Just before his death in 50 A.D., Philo wrote, "the Logos of the living God is the bond of everything, holding all things together and binding all the parts, and preventing them from being

---

[34] http://www.thebiblejourney.org/more-resources/talks/whats-in-a-word/

dissolved and separated."[35] This certainly sounds like Paul's words to the church at Colossae. Paul wrote, "He is the image of the invisible God, the firstborn of all creation. For by Him all things were created, both in the heavens and on earth, visible and invisible, whether thrones or dominions or rulers or authorities— all things have been created through Him and for Him. He is before all things, and in Him all things hold together."[36]

While Philo's thoughts seem to be right in line with Christ being God in the flesh, we must remember that Philo did not have a Trinitarian view of God. He saw the word (logos) as subordinate to Almighty God.

However, the Greek and Jewish philosophies of the day give stunning background to John's choice of the word "Word" in this chapter. Not only is the Word John that refers to a personal being, not a force, but the being took on human flesh and dwelt among men showing the glory of the one true and living God. Indeed, this Logos, Jesus Christ, did give meaning and purpose to all things and was the ultimate reality.

How fitting it is to give this name to Jesus Christ. He is God's living Word. Whatever God wants to say, He says through the Word, the Son of God. Being the Logos, or full expression of God, Christ revealed God's nature and character to man.

While the Greek word "logos" is used 330 times in the New Testament, there are only six times in most modern translations that the "W" is capitalized indicating a reference to the person of

---

[35] http://www.thebiblejourney.org/more-resources/talks/whats-in-a-word/
[36] Colossians 1:15-17, NASB.

Christ. The determination of these Scriptures referring specifically to Christ over so many others seems to be the translators determining that the context of these verses warrant such a designation.

Here are the six passages in which the Greek word "Logos" is used with the capital "W" indicating a reference to Christ as the Word of God:

John 1:1 (3x)

*In the beginning was the **Word**, and the **Word** was with God, and the **Word** was God.*

John 1:14

*And the **Word** became flesh, and dwelt among us, and we saw His glory, glory as of the only begotten from the Father, full of grace and truth.*

1 John 1:1

*What was from the beginning, what we have heard, what we have seen with our eyes, what we have looked at and touched with our hands, concerning the **Word** of Life—*

Revelation 19:13

*He is clothed with a robe dipped in blood, and His name is called The **Word** of God.*

Each of these uses of the capital letter "W" to make a distinction in the text is found in the writings of the Apostle John. This makes sense given the connection of Ephesus with Heraclitus and John.

The Word of the Lord

There is one more implication of Christ being the Logos or Word of God. There is an Aramaic word, *memra,* that is used in the Targum, the Jewish translations and commentaries on the Old Testament. This word, *memra,* means, "The Word of the Lord."

As the Hebrew language began to fall out of use after the return from exile, Aramaic began to be widely used. Jewish scholars would translate and interpret the Old Testament in these Targums. The Jews had such a reverence for the divine name that they would avoid spelling it out or even using it in copies of Scripture or even Targums.

What we find is that when there are physical manifestations of God used in the text of the Old Testament, the Jewish scholars would use the word *memra,* or, The Word of the Lord. It is used hundreds of times in the Targums.

Kyle Pope writes, "As early as the first century A.D. interpretations (or paraphrases) of religious passages known as *Targums,* began to be written down in Aramaic for Jews who no longer spoke Hebrew. In the *Targums* the Jews used the Aramaic word *memra* meaning "word" as a personal manifestation of the presence of God. When Exodus 19:17 tells us that—"Moses brought the people out of the camp to meet with God" the Targums interpret this to mean that he brought them—"to meet the Word (*memra*) of the Lord."[37]

------

[37] Kyle Pope, "In the Beginning was the Word: A Study of the Logos Doctrine" www.ancientroadpublications.com Accessed April 11, 2019. http://ancientroadpublications.com/Studies/BiblicalStudies/Logos.ht ml

Jonathan Bernis, President of Jewish Voice Ministries International, writes, "Targum Onkelos, which was completed within the first four centuries after Jesus lived, says that Adam and Eve heard the Memra of the Lord walking in the Garden. Memra, according to the Jewish Encyclopedia, means "The Word." The Word, then, is not just a random statement of some minor aspect of God's character. It is a person who is one with God yet has His own being. This person is Messiah, who walked with God in the Garden of Eden and later came to us in human form to save His people."[38]

The exact phrase, "the word of the Lord" is used in 239 verses of the Old Testament. More specifically, the exact phrase, "the word of the Lord came to" is used in 93 verses. Some of these verses describe the same event, so it is improper to assume these are 93 different occasions. Still, it is possible that "the word of the Lord" is referring to a person just as John's use of The Word (Logos), refers to Christ.

James Moffatt writes, "In the Old Testament, and particularly in the prophetic writings, the idea of the "Word of the Lord" as such a vehicle is of frequent occurrence; in poetical passages that "Word" is sometimes all but personified. The process is carried farther in the popular Aramaic paraphrases of the Old Testament known as Targums, in which reverence forbids the assumption of direct contact between God and the world, and the "Memra," or "Word of God," is supplied as *the* vehicle *of intermediate* action in *God's*

---

[38] Jonathan Bernis, "Finding Jesus in the Old Testament" www.charismamag.com Accessed April 19, 2016.
http://www.charismamag.com/spirit/bible-study/15023-finding-jesus-in-the-old-testament

dealings with men. Thus <u>Gen. 3:8</u> in the Targum reads, "They heard the voice of the Memra of the Lord God walking in the Garden." The parallelism of the first verses of the Prologue with the opening *verses* of *Genesis seems* to prove that John is moulding his thought of the creative Logos upon this Old Testament conception of the Word as the vehicle of Divine activity."[39]

I will offer one simple line of logic in support of this idea.

Genesis 1:1

In the beginning God created the heavens and the earth.

We have already discussed that "God" in this verse is the **plural** Hebrew title Elohim, indicating the Godhead.

John 1:1-2

In the beginning was the Word, and the Word was with God, and the Word was God. 2 He was in the beginning with God.

This verse also presents a plurality because the Word was **with** God. So, if Christ is The Word, He is present at Creation.

John 1:3,10

3 All things came into being through Him, and apart from Him nothing came into being that has come into being. 10 He was in the world, and the world was made through Him, and the world did not know Him.

---

[39] W.E. Read, "Christ The Logos-The Word of God" www.ministrymagazine.org Accessed June 30, 2016. https://www.ministrymagazine.org/archive/1958/08/christ-the-logos-the-word-of-god

John goes on to explain plainly that Christ was, in fact, the agent of Creation. Other New Testament texts support this.

1 Corinthians 8:6

*6 yet for us there is but one God, the Father, from whom are all things and we exist for Him; and one Lord, **Jesus Christ, by whom are all things**, and we exist through Him.*

Colossians 1:13-16

*13 For He rescued us from the domain of darkness, and transferred us to the kingdom of His beloved Son, 14 in whom we have redemption, the forgiveness of sins. 15 He is the image of the invisible God, the **firstborn of all creation**. 16 **For by Him all things were created**, both in the heavens and on earth, visible and invisible, whether thrones or dominions or rulers or authorities — all things have been created through Him and for Him.*

Hebrews 1:2

*2 in these last days has spoken to us in His Son, whom He appointed heir of all things, **through whom also He made the world**.*

Psalm 33:6

*6 By **the word of the Lord** the heavens were made, And by the breath of His mouth all their host.*

So, if we have already established that Christ was the agent of creation, and He was present in the beginning with God, would it not stand to reason that Christ is also "the word of the Lord" by whom the heavens were made?

A.W. Tozer wrote, "The teachings of the New Testament is that God created the world by the Logos, the Word, and the Word is identified with the second person of the Godhead who was present in the world even before He became incarnate in human nature."[40]

---

[40] A.W. Tozer, *The Knowledge of the Holy* (San Francisco: Harper Collins, 1992), 117.

John M. Burris

Chapter Five

Setting Out the Pieces

"The art of simplicity is a puzzle of complexity."

- Douglas Horton

Not everyone works puzzles the way I do. The first thing I do, when sitting down to work a jigsaw puzzle, is set out all the pieces. I would rather have access to the pieces than to keep turning over the same pieces while mixed up in the box, looking for just the right piece. Often, patterns emerge that offers a place to begin.

So, we come to the puzzle of, "Where was the Son of God in the thousands of years before Bethlehem and what was He doing?" Perhaps it will help us to set out the pieces we have so far...

- There is an overarching plan of God that has existed since before the creation of the world that has in mind God relating to His creation. (Rev. 13:8)

- The Bible records that God appeared to people in The Old Testament. (Genesis 18:1-3, Genesis 32:24-25, 28-30)

- The Bible also declares that no one has seen God at any time. (John 1:18) Yet, the second part of that verse reveals that the only begotten Son has explained Him.

- The truth of the Trinity, i.e. Godhead or triune nature of God, allows us to conclude that Jesus Christ is God (Heb. 1:3, Col. 2:9, John12:45, Phil. 2:6) and that Jesus Christ is eternal. (Heb. 1:8)

- The truth of the Trinity also allows us to conclude that God is relational in His very nature.

- The use of the plural in the Hebrew language supports the idea of a Godhead, or Trinity, one God in three persons. (Genesis 1:26)

- Christ, in the New Testament, exhibited emotions that allowed Him to identify with man. These emotions were love, sorrow, joy, righteous anger. He displayed the character of God to human beings.

- Christ, being eternal, has always been. He did not show up one day in a manger at Bethlehem. (John 1:12, Heb. 1:2, Micah 5:2-4, John 8:58, John 17:5)

- Being the Logos, The Word of God, Christ has given real meaning and purpose to all things that have existed (John 1:1-18)

Most people that I know, complete the border of a puzzle before trying to fill in the rest of the puzzle. In doing so, what seems most helpful are to find the corner pieces. These pieces seem to help establish the framework for the entire puzzle. So, of the pieces we have gathered so far, there are some key "corner pieces" that lead us to begin to understand what the puzzle may look like.

- Christ is completely Divine.

- Christ has always existed.

- Christ is the image of God. He reveals the Father.

- Christ is relational. The Christ of the New Testament does not act differently prior to the New Testament.

These "corner" pieces lead me to an assertion that I will attempt to support throughout this book.

My Fundamental assertion…

Jesus Christ, the Son of God is the distinct, but essential person of the Godhead who relates to man in sight, speech and presence in human form. Christ has always been the personification of the nature and character of God. (2 Cor. 4:6) (John 1:18)

This assertion is not a completely new idea but finds confirmation in much conservative scholarship.

Jonathan Edwards: "When we read in sacred history what God did from time to time towards his church and people, and what he said to them, and how he revealed himself to them, we are to understand it especially of the second Person of the Trinity. When we read of God's appearing after the Fall, from time to time, in some visible form or outward symbol of his presence, we are ordinarily, if not universally, to understand it of the second Person of the Trinity." [41]

The early church father Tertullian put it like this: "It was the Son who judged men from the beginning, destroying that lofty tower,

---

[41] David Murray, *Jesus on Every Page* (Nashville: Thomas Nelson Publishers, 2013), 76.

and confounding their languages, punishing the whole world with a flood of waters, and raining fire and brimstone upon Sodom and Gomorrah . . . for he always descended to hold converse with men, from Adam even to the patriarchs and prophets, in visions, in dreams, in mirrors, in dark sentences, always preparing his way from the beginning: neither was it possible, that God who conversed with men upon earth, could be any other than that Word which was to be made flesh."[42]

Dr. John Walvoord, former President of Dallas Theological Seminary, wrote, "It is safe to assume that every visible manifestation of God in bodily form in the Old Testament is to be identified with the Lord Jesus Christ."[43]

John Calvin writes, "Holy men of old knew God only by beholding Him in His Son as in a mirror (cf. 2 Cor. 3:18). When I say this, I mean that God has never Manifested Himself to men in any other way than through the Son, that is, His sole wisdom, light, and truth. From this fountain Adam, Noah, Abraham, Isaac, Jacob, and others drank all that they had of heavenly teaching. From the same fountain, all the prophets have also drawn every heavenly oracle that they have given forth."[44]

---

[42] Murray, 76-77.
[43] John F. Walvoord, *Jesus Christ Our Lord* (Chicago: Moody Publishers, 1969), 54.
[44] Murray, 75.

Chapter Six

From the Lips of the Almighty

"Truly, truly, I say to you, before Abraham was born, I am."

- *Jesus*

Thankfully, my fundamental assertion of Christ relating to man in sight, speech and presence doesn't depend solely on my ingenuity or intellect, or the intellect of the many brilliant scholars who have studied the Scriptures so diligently over the centuries. We have the very words of Christ that testify of His divinity and pre-existence.

Christ's Divinity

John 5:39-46

39 You search the Scriptures because you think that in them you have eternal life; it is these that testify about Me; 40 and you are unwilling to come to Me so that you may have life. 41 I do not receive glory from men; 42 but I know you, that you do not have the love of God in yourselves. 43 I have come in My Father's name, and you do not receive Me; if another comes in his own name, you will receive him. 44 How can you believe, when you receive glory from one another, and you do not seek the glory that is from the one and only God? 45 Do not think that I will accuse you before the Father; the one who accuses you is Moses, in whom you have *set your hope. **46** For if you believed Moses, you would believe Me, for he wrote about Me.*

Here, Christ is speaking to the Pharisees, the religious leaders of the day. The Pharisees made it their aim (and also their boast) to strictly adhere to the Old Testament Law. This was not merely the Ten Commandments that God gave to Moses. In addition, they had devised a whole system of laws, 613 laws in fact, 368 negative laws (Thou shalt not's) and 248 positive laws (Thou shalt's).[45]

The Pharisees had indeed searched the Scriptures looking for every word that could be made into a law. According to Christ's reproach of them, their intent was to find eternal life in adherence to the letter of every command of the Old Testament. Instead, He declares that the Scriptures testify about Him. Obviously, the Scriptures that Christ refers to is the Old Testament.

Furthermore, He declares that they must come to Him in order to have eternal life (v.40). And, to remove any doubt as to His divinity, Christ declares that Moses wrote about Him.

Mark 14:61-64

61 But He kept silent and did not answer. Again the high priest was questioning Him, and saying to Him, "Are You the Christ, the Son of the Blessed One?" 62 And Jesus said, "I am; and you shall see the Son of Man sitting at the right hand of Power, and coming with the clouds of heaven." 63 Tearing his clothes, the high priest said, "What further need do we have

---

[45] Joseph M. Stowell, *Fan the Flame: Living Out Your First Love for Christ* (Chicago: Moody Press, 1986), 52. (parentheses mine)

*of witnesses? **64** You have heard the blasphemy; how does it seem to you?"
And they all condemned Him to be deserving of death.*

As Christ is soon to face His certain death, He finds Himself again in front of the religious leaders. They are attempting to find a reason under Jewish Law to put Him to death. After a parade of false witnesses and conflicting testimony, Christ makes no argument for Himself. This fact alone fulfills the prophecy of the Messiah in Isaiah 53:7, *"He was oppressed and He was afflicted, yet He did not open His mouth."*

But, when the question was asked of Him directly about who He was, He responded in a powerful way. When Jesus utters the response, "I am", He is not simply responding to the question. He is powerfully declaring that He is Divine.

J. Oswald Sanders writes, "No less astounding are the claims He made in His 'I AM' utterances. These are undoubted assumptions of deity, as is His claim to possess the divine resources to meet all human need."[46]

This same declaration of deity was given in the garden of Gethsemane the night before Christ was crucified.

John 18:4-6

*4 So Jesus, knowing all the things that were coming upon Him, went forth and *said to them, "Whom do you seek?" 5 They answered Him, "Jesus the Nazarene." He *said to them, "I am He." And Judas also, who*

---

[46] J. Oswald Sanders, *The Incomparable Christ* (Chicago: Moody Press, 1971), 70.

was betraying Him, was standing with them. 6 So when He said to them, "I am He," they drew back and fell to the ground.

The response of those gathered in the garden that dark night is no less stunning. They drew back and fell to the ground. Edmund Clowney speaks of this when he writes, "When Jesus declared, 'I am', in the garden of Gethsemane, those who had come to arrest Him fell backward to the ground. Every word of the Lord is filled with power. God speaks and it is done, He commands and it stands fast. But when God speaks His own name, the power of His word takes on a special significance."[47]

Christ's Pre-Existence

John 1:15

15 John testified about Him and cried out, saying, "This was He of whom I said, 'He who comes after me has a higher rank than I, for He existed before me.'"

Here, John the Baptist is speaking of Christ. He declares that Jesus existed before Himself. The reason this is significant is that John the Baptist was born at least six months prior to Jesus. We read in Luke's Gospel that in Elizabeth's sixth month of her pregnancy with John the Baptist, the angel Gabriel appeared to Mary (while she was still a virgin) and announced to her that she would conceive a son.[48]

---

[47] Edmund Clowney, *The Unfolding Mystery: Discovering Christ in the Old Testament* (Phillipsburg: P & R Publishing, 1988), 92.
[48] Luke 1:26-31 NASB

So, if John the Baptist declared that Christ existed before himself, it could only mean that he was referring to His pre-existence.

John 3:13

13 No one has ascended into heaven, but He who descended from heaven: the Son of Man.

Here, Christ is speaking with Nicodemus, one of the Pharisees. Christ tells Nicodemus that He has descended from Heaven. Notice that this occurrence was well before His death, burial and resurrection. So Christ could not be referring to a glorified, post-resurrection state.

Also, this declaration sets Jesus apart from all other men who are born of women. Earlier in their conversation, Christ told Nicodemus that *"unless one was born of water and the Spirit, he cannot enter into the kingdom of God."*[49]

John 8:23

23 And He was saying to them, "You are from below, I am from above; you are of this world, I am not of this world.

Here, Christ is speaking in the Temple during the Feast of Tabernacles. He declares to all who were gathered (which would have been a great multitude of Jews since the Feast of Tabernacles was a pilgrimage feast). In declaring He is from above, Jesus is claiming that He has pre-existed prior to being born of Mary in Bethlehem.

---

[49] John 3:5 NASB

John 8:56-59

56 Your father Abraham rejoiced to see My day, and he saw it and was glad." 57 So the Jews said to Him, "You are not yet fifty years old, and have You seen Abraham?" 58 Jesus said to them, "Truly, truly, I say to you, before Abraham was born, I am."

This is an astounding text. Christ tells a group of Jews about the importance of obeying His words. The Jews found it particularly difficult to accept this teaching because they were not convinced that he had the authority to make such a claim. Responding to them, He tells them that Abraham rejoiced in seeing Christ. This must have sounded absolutely ridiculous if only hearing from a human perspective. But, if one were to believe that Christ was divine and eternal, it would make perfect sense.

John Walvoord writes, "When Christ said, 'Before Abraham came to be [Greek, genesthai], I am [Greek, eimi]' (literal trans.). He was not only claiming to have existed before Abraham, but He was claiming to be the eternal I AM, that is, the Jehovah of the Old Testament."[50] It is also worth noting that this passage includes what we have already discussed as the divine title of "I AM." Thus, this passage also supports the divinity of Christ.

John 16:28

28 I came forth from the Father and have come into the world; I am leaving the world again and going to the Father."

---

[50] John F. Walvoord, *Jesus Christ Our Lord* (Chicago: Moody Publishers, 1969), 24.

Here again, Christ declares that He had another residence prior to His earthly existence, one to which He would also return. We must conclude that He existed prior to the manger in Bethlehem and that His abode was with the Father.

John 17:5

5 Now, Father, glorify Me together with Yourself, with the glory which I had with You before the world was.

Here, Christ is praying fervently in the garden of Gethsemane before He is to be delivered over into the hands of the Pharisees, eventually to be crucified.

This passage gives even more clarity to some of the other claims of Christ. With this statement, Christ removes any doubt as to where and when He pre-existed. According to this passage, He existed with the Father before the world ever began. In addition, the passage also reveals that Christ possessed glory from before the foundation of the world. In this sense, this passage also affirms Christ's divinity.

Obviously, there are many other passages that give ample evidence that Christ existed from the very beginning. John 1:1-4, Hebrews 1:1-2 and Revelation 13:8 are just three other examples. But, the intent of this chapter was to look at the very words of Christ to see what He said of Himself.

C.S. Lewis wrote, "A man who was merely a man and said the sort of things Jesus said would not be a great moral teacher. He would either be a lunatic -- on the level with a man who said he was a poached egg -- or else he would be the Devil of Hell. You must make your choice. Either this man was, and is, the Son of God:

or else a madman or something worse. You can shut him up for a fool, you can spit at Him and kill Him as a demon; or you can fall at His feet and call Him Lord and God. But let us not come with some patronizing nonsense about Him being a great human teacher. He has not left that open to us. He did not intend to"[51]

Other New Testament Evidence for The Pre-incarnate Christ

One of the most fascinating events of the New Testament happens between just three people on a road from Jerusalem to Emmaus. Jesus has just been crucified and those who had hoped for The Messiah to usher in the kingdom of God had been all but lost. Two men, who we at least know were hoping that Jesus would redeem Israel, were discussing all that had taken place in the recent past. Luke 24:15-16 says, *"And it came about that while they were conversing and discussing, Jesus Himself approached and began traveling with them. But their eyes were prevented from recognizing Him."*[52]

Jesus allows the men to relate what they know of what has taken place, but continues to veil Himself. And then, Luke records an incredible verse. *"And beginning with Moses and with all the prophets, He explained to them the things concerning Himself in all the Scriptures."*[53] If only we had an outline of that talk! Jesus used the Old Testament Scripture to reveal to these two men about His redeeming work as Messiah.

---

[51] C.S. Lewis, *Mere Christianity* (New York: MacMillan Co., 1953), 41.
[52] Luke 24:15-16, NASB
[53] Luke 24:27, NASB

John 1:45

45 Philip *found Nathanael and *said to him, "We have found Him of whom Moses in the Law and also the Prophets wrote — Jesus of Nazareth, the son of Joseph."

Hebrews 11:26-27

26 considering the reproach of Christ greater riches than the treasures of Egypt; for he was looking to the reward. 27 By faith he left Egypt, not fearing the wrath of the king; for he endured, as seeing Him who is unseen.

The writer of Hebrews is speaking of Moses as one who saw Christ.

1 Peter 1:10-12

10 As to this salvation, the prophets who prophesied of the grace that would come to you made careful searches and inquiries, 11 seeking to know what person or time the Spirit of Christ within them was indicating as He predicted the sufferings of Christ and the glories to follow. 12 It was revealed to them that they were not serving themselves, but you, in these things which now have been announced to you through those who preached the gospel to you by the Holy Spirit sent from heaven — things into which angels long to look.

According to this passage in 1 Peter, Peter is declaring that the Holy Spirit, the third person of the Trinity, revealed to the prophets about Christ.

Chapter Seven

The Angel of the Lord

"The Angel of the Lord was not merely 'an angel'; He was a theophany- an appearance of the second Person of the Trinity in visible and bodily form before the Incarnation."

– F. Duane Lindsey

E very puzzle has some pieces that have a strange shape. Just by looking at them alone, it is difficult to see how they fit into the overall picture.

The Angel of the Lord is one such piece to the puzzle of the glorious mystery of the pre-incarnate Christ. Is The Angel of the Lord simply a messenger angel sent from God to communicate directly with some of the people of the Old Testament? Or, is The Angel of the Lord the title that was given to Christ in His pre-incarnate form?

Our simple minds often want to make God simple so we can understand Him. I am learning more and more that while God is simple enough for me to understand what I need to know, I will not know the fullness of His being and character until I am in Heaven with Him.

Don Stewart identifies three major views that have been put forth as to the exact identity of the Angel of the Lord.

1. A mighty angel who acted as the special representative of the LORD.

2. God the Father assuming a human body.

3. God the Son, taking a body for a short period of time.[54]

I would like to add a fourth possibility to the list of views. Although, it may not be much different than the third view, I believe the difference is important.

4. The Second Person of the Trinity, Christ, the Son of God in His pre-incarnate form.

My problem with the third view is the phrase, "for a short period of time." Keeping in mind my fundamental assertion…

Jesus Christ, the Son of God is the distinct, but essential person of the Godhead who relates to man in sight, speech and presence in human form. Christ has always been the personification of the nature and character of God. (2 Cor. 4:6) (John 1:18)

I do not see Christ appearing as The Angel of the Lord to be like running into a closet in Heaven and throwing on a man suit so that He can bring a human being a message.

However, I do believe that this was a pre-incarnate form, not human flesh. While the form may have taken on the appearance,

---

[54] Don Stewart, "Who is The Angel of the Lord in the Old Testament" www.blueletterbible.org Accessed June 24, 2016. https://www.blueletterbible.org/faq/don_stewart/don_stewart_26.cfm

and perhaps even some of the qualities of human flesh, Christ's full and complete sacrifice for sin was only accomplished by Him taking on literal, human flesh, being born of a virgin and experiencing the excruciating death on the cross for our sin. So, Christ's pre-incarnate state, while a bodily form and substance, is not the same as the "flesh" He took on when He was born of Mary.

Defining the Term

The Hebrew word for angel means simply "messenger." Our minds are muddied with images that have been given to us by well-meaning Sunday School curriculum artists, pop culture and Hollywood filmmakers. When we hear the word angel, certain images come to mind: pudgy toga-clad babies floating on clouds and playing harps, the gentle elderly Clarence from *It's a Wonderful Life*, or John Travolta with enormous white wings in *City of Angels*, or any number of other depictions of angels. We must rid ourselves of such presuppositions. In fact, I would imagine, from a Biblical perspective, that a true description of an angel would be rather intimidating, even frightening. I believe they are fierce, powerful created beings who bring praise to God and, yet, execute His judgment at His command.

In the case of the angel of the Lord, the emphasis is on the aspect of being a messenger rather than the actual physical appearance. If the physical appearance would have been extremely important, God would have let us know through His Word.

Vern Poythress writes of this Hebrew word (*malak*), translated most frequently as "angel", "The word in itself does not determine what sort of personage is designated, whether divine or human or angelic, in our modern sense of the word *angel*. For example,

Malachi uses the same word… to describe prophetically the coming of John the Baptist as a "messenger." Also in Malachi, the priest is "the messenger of the Lord of hosts."[55]

As to the title "Lord", Michael Barrett has an interesting explanation. He writes, "I suggest that interpreting the word 'Lord' as being in apposition to the word 'angel' best explains and accounts for the mystery of this person. (Remember that apposition is a renaming of a noun, usually in a more specific manner.) In other words, the Angel of the Lord is the Angel *who* is the Lord."[56]

Barrett goes on to write, "The significance of this identification is profound when we recognize that the word "Lord" refers to Jehovah. Jehovah, of course, is that unique name of the One true and living God. Therefore, to equate the Angel with Jehovah irrefutably proves His Deity… Further, this interpretation is distinctively Christological in that by identifying God as the Second Person of the Trinity, it accounts for the times the Angel seems to be distinct from God the Father. Nevertheless, Scripture does makes clear that the Angel is Christ, who is God."[57]

So, quite literally, the Angel of the Lord means simply, The Messenger of Jehovah. Or, using Barrett's apposition device, The Messenger who is Jehovah. And, according to my fundamental

---

[55] Vern Poythress, *Theophany: A Biblical Theology of God's Appearing* (Wheaton: Crossway Books, 2018), 68-69.
[56] Michael P. V. Barrett, *Beginning at Moses: A Guide to Finding Christ in the Old Testament* (Greenville: Ambassador-Emerald International, 1999), 149.
[57] Barrett, 150.

assertion, this would be the Second Person of the Trinity, Christ, the Son of God.

Further Evidence

David Murray lists six proofs of the deity of the Angel of The Lord…

1. He claims divine authority. He speaks as only God can and swears by Himself as only God can. (Genesis 16:10; 22:15-16)

2. He is a distinct divine person. At times He is identified with Jehovah; at other times He is carefully distinguished, highlighting the distinct individual persons of the Godhead. (2 Samuel 24:16; Zechariah 1:12)

3. He exhibits divine attributes. For example, Hagar realized that this Angel had an omniscient awareness of her personal circumstances: her name, occupation, and location. (Genesis 16:7-8) He also knew her current status of being pregnant and the gender of the child, and He even directed the selection of the child's name. (Genesis 16:11) No wonder she described Him as "the-God-Who-Sees." (Genesis 16:13)

4. He performs divine actions. He utters curses of divine judgment, judges, and redeems sinners. (Judges 5:23; 2 Kings 19:35; Genesis 48:15-16)

5. He receives divine homage. The Angel is to be treated as God. (Exodus 23:20-21) He receives sacrifice from Gideon and is called Jehovah-Shalom, "The LORD-Is-Peace." (Judges 6:20-21,24)

6. He is identified as God. The literal translation of Hagar's words in Genesis 16: 13 is: "Then she called [the] name of the LORD, the One speaking to her, 'You [are the] God of appearance,' for she said, 'Have even I seen here the One who sees me?'" In Genesis 22, the Angel of the Lord and the Lord are spoken of as one and the same person. (Genesis 22:12, 15-16) In Genesis 31, the Angel identifies Himself as God: "Then the Angel of God spoke to me in a dream, saying, 'Jacob . . . I am the God of Bethel.'" (Genesis 31:11-13) After speaking with the Angel, Samson's father, Manoah, exclaimed to his wife: "We shall surely die, because we have seen God!" (Judges 13:21-22)[58]

Murray concludes by writing, "In summary, because this Angel is God, and God reveals Himself through His Son, we must conclude that this angel is the Son of God in human form."[59]

The Angel of The Lord in The Old Testament

The phrase, "the Angel of the Lord", or "the Angel of God" appears in 62 verses in the Old Testament in 11 different books. These 62 verses represent 25 separate occasions or events where the Angel of The Lord related to human beings directly.

I believe that when you see the phrase "the angel of the Lord" in the Old Testament, you are to understand it as being the second person of the trinity, Jesus Christ.

---

[58] David Murray, *Jesus on Every Page* (Nashville: Thomas Nelson Publishers, 2013), 78-79.
[59] Murray, 80.

Conservative scholarship holds this position. Consider the following comments.

"John F. Walvoord, highly respected for his exposition of the prophetic sections of the Scriptures and former president of Dallas Theological Seminary, lists four arguments supporting the conclusion that the appearances of the Angel of Jehovah represent 'Christophanies' or visible appearances of our Lord Jesus Christ prior to His incarnation.

1) The Second Person is the Visible God of the New Testament.

2) The Angel of Jehovah of the Old Testament no longer appears after the incarnation of Christ.

3) Both the Angel of Jehovah and Christ are sent by the Father.

4) The Angel of Jehovah could not be either the Father or the Holy Spirit for the Father and the Spirit are invisible to man.

Dr. Walvoord concludes, "there is not a single valid reason to deny that the Angel of Jehovah is the Second Person, every known fact pointing to His identification as the Christ of the New Testament."[60]

Warren Wiersbe comments, "In the Old Testament, the "angel of the Lord" is generally interpreted to be the Lord Himself, who occasionally came to earth (a theophany) to deliver an important

---

[60] Precept Austin. "Who is The Angel of The Lord?" www.preceptaustin.org Accessed June 26, 2016. http://www.preceptaustin.org/angel_of_the_lord.htm

message. It was probably the Lord Jesus Christ, the second Person of the Godhead, in a temporary pre-incarnation appearance."[61]

J. Vernon McGee says, "I believe that the angel of the Lord is none other than the pre-incarnate Christ."[62]

John MacArthur writes, "The Angel of the Lord, who does not appear after the birth of Christ, is often identified as the pre-incarnate Christ."[63]

Justin Martyr declared, "Our Christ conversed with Moses out of the bush, in the appearance of fire. And Moses received great strength from Christ, who spake to him in the appearance of fire."[64]

Irenaeus wrote, "The Scripture is full of the Son of God's appearing: sometimes to talk and eat with Abraham, at other times to instruct Noah about the measures of the ark; at another time to seek Adam; at another time to bring down judgment upon Sodom; then again, to direct Jacob in the way; and again, to converse with Moses out of the bush."[65]

---

[61] Warren Wiersbe, *Be Available (Judges): Accepting the Challenge to Confront the Enemy* (Colorado Springs: David C. Cook, 1994), 25.
[62] J. Vernon McGee, *Thru the Bible Commentary vol. 3* (Nashville: Thomas Nelson Publishers, 1983), 341.
[63] John MacArthur, The MacArthur Study Bible (Nashville: Thomas Nelson Publishers, 2013), 37.
[64] Precept Austin. "Who is The Angel of The Lord?" www.preceptaustin.org Accessed June 26, 2016.
http://www.preceptaustin.org/angel_of_the_lord.htm
[65] Precept Austin. "Who is The Angel of The Lord?" www.preceptaustin.org Accessed June 26, 2016.
http://www.preceptaustin.org/angel_of_the_lord.htm

Henry Law, in his book, <u>Gleanings from the Book of Life</u>, wrote, "We here learn that Jesus is "the Angel of the Lord." The voice announced, "I am God," and the appearance exhibited a human form. Who can be both God and man but Jesus? The Father never appeared as man. The Holy Spirit never thus condescended. But the blessed Jesus, anticipating the time when earth should claim Him as its child, not infrequently assumed our form. Therefore, without hesitation, we receive "the Angel of the Lord" as Jesus the incarnate God."[66]

It is important to note that the phrase, "The Angel of the Lord" in the Old Testament does not always signify an appearance. There are times when the angel of the Lord is mentioned as if recalling a prior experience or describing the action of the angel of the Lord.

There are literally hundreds of other references that could be made that would indeed affirm that The Angel of the Lord was a pre-incarnate appearance of Christ.

This truth has made so much sense to me and given me such encouragement as to the power and divinity of Christ.

Scriptural Evidence of The Angel of the Lord

The Angel of The Lord

Genesis 16:7, 9, 10, 11- appearing to Hagar

Genesis 22:11, 15 - appearing to Abraham and Isaac

---

[66] Precept Austin. "Who is The Angel of The Lord?" www.preceptaustin.org Accessed June 26, 2016. http://www.preceptaustin.org/angel_of_the_lord.htm

Exodus 3:2 - appearing to Moses at the burning bush

Numbers 22:22-27, 31-35 - appearing to Balaam

Judges 2:1, 4 - announces judgment on Israelites

Judges 5:23 - spoken of in the song of Deborah and Barak

Judges 6:11-12, 21-22 - appearing to Gideon

Judges 13:3, 13-18, 20-21- appearing to Samson's parents *

2 Samuel 24:16 - appearing at the threshing floor of Araunah

1 Kings 19:7 - appearing to Elijah

2 Kings 1:3, 15 - speaking to Elijah

2 Kings 19:35 - struck down 185,000 Assyrians

1 Chronicles 21:12, 15-16, 18, 30 - appearing at the threshing floor of Araunah (duplicate event)

Psalm 37:4 - encamps around those who fear Him

Psalm 35:5-6 - contending with those who are against the Lord

Isaiah- 37:36 - struck down 185,000 Assyrians (duplicate event)

Zechariah 1:11, 12 - appearing to Zechariah among the myrtle trees (seen in a vision)

Zechariah 3:1, 5-6 - appearing to Joshua the High Priest (seen in a vision)

Zechariah 12:8 - house of David compared to the Angel of the Lord

The Angel of God

Genesis 21:17 – appearing to Hagar

Genesis 31:11 - appearing to Jacob

Exodus 14:19 - going before the camp of Israel

Judges 6:20 - appearing to Gideon

Judges 13:6, 9 - appearing to Samson's parents*

1 Samuel 29:9 - David described as like an angel of God

2 Samuel 14:17, 20 - David described as like an angel of God

2 Samuel 19:27- David described as like an angel of God (duplicate event)

*Notice that both The Angel of the Lord and The Angel of God are referred to in the accounts of Samson's parents.

Chapter Eight

Christophanies in The Old Testament

"If ever the divine appeared on earth, it was in the person of Christ."

– *Johann Wolfgang von Goethe*

A *Christophany* is a visible appearance of the pre-incarnate Christ in the Old Testament. Many scholars use the term theophany to refer to the appearance of God in human form. I choose to use the term *Christophany* because I believe that Christ, being completely God, is the image of the invisible God. He makes God visible.

Scholars have long used the term "theophany" to define an appearance of God. However, there is much debate as to the particulars of just how God appears. In my opinion, the debate is unnecessary. Whether it is called a *theophany* or a *Christophany*, it is still the manifestation of the Second Person of the Trinity doing what He has always done, relating to man.

In this way, the Angel of the Lord discussed in the previous chapter would be considered a Christophany. While there may be some doubt in the minds of some as to the appearances of the Angel of the Lord being Christ, there are other passages that are rather obvious as to the literal presence of Christ.

Apart from The Angel of the Lord, I have identified 22 pre-incarnate appearances of Christ in 10 Old Testament books. These Christophanies include language like, "The Lord appeared", "The Lord came down", "The Lord stood" and those who "walked with God" (particularly Enoch and Noah who the context gives us reason to believe that the walking was not figurative as it is for us today). These appearances do not include the presence of the Lord, the glory of the Lord, or the Lord appearing in dreams or visions. While these could be considered Christophanies, it seemed more appropriate to include only the more obvious instances.

In all, there are 39 passages in the Old Testament that I have identified where there is an appearance of the pre-incarnate Christ. In all of these, He is identified as The Angel of the Lord, The Captain of the Lord's Host, God Himself, the word of the Lord, the Lord or even places where He is present but not named. This list may not be completely exhaustive. I tried to only identify passages that only dealt with an appearance of Christ. For certain, there are many more passages that are types, allusions or even descriptive of His pre-incarnate characteristics, most notable speaking. But, for the pre-incarnate Christ to speak, does not necessarily mean He was physically present.

James Borland gives a good definition of the term Christophany as, "unsought, intermittent and temporary, visible and audible manifestations of God the Son in human form, by which God communicated something to certain conscious human beings on earth prior to the birth of Jesus Christ."[67]

The only word in the definition that does not sit well with me is the word temporary. It is difficult for me to think of Christ in any way to be temporary. I believe Borland's point, however, is to distinguish from the form Christ took in Old Testament appearances versus His incarnate state as described in the New Testament. This is evident as he begins to narrow the scope of Biblical evidence for Christophanies. He writes, "Christophanies may be differentiated from dreams and visions, the pillar of cloud of the wilderness journeys, the Shekinah glory of the tabernacle and the Temple, and even from the incarnation of Christ, His resurrection appearances, and His second coming."[68]

I would add, that while these would be different from a Christophany, especially the ones I am attempting to identify in this book, they are still to be considered as the activity of God.

For example, in Exodus when the Lord communicates with Moses in such passages as Exodus 10:1, "Then the Lord said to Moses...", Exodus 11:1, "Then the Lord said to Moses..." and Exodus 12:1, "Then the Lord said to Moses...", I believe it is Christ who is speaking. Christ is communicating to Moses what the Godhead wants him to know. The reason it is not a Christophany is that, as far as we can know, Christ may not have been bodily present. It may have only been a voice. By the way, from the time

---

[67]James Borland, *Christ in the Old Testament: Old Testament Appearances of Christ in Human Form* (Fern, Ross-shire: Christian Focus Publications, 2010), 17.
[68] Borland, 17.

that God called Moses from the burning bush (which was Christ in the midst of the bush), Exodus continually records the consistent voice of the Lord to Moses. He was totally dependent on the voice of the Lord.

We can be assured that Moses not only heard the voice of the Lord but saw Him as well. "By faith he left Egypt, not fearing the wrath of the king; for he endured, as seeing Him who is unseen."[69]

Michael Barrett concurs, "I suppose one of the questions I am asked most frequently is how much of Christ the Old Testament saints really knew. My typical response is that I don't know how much they knew, but I do know how much they should have known in the light of God's revelation to them. In addition to all the things God said to them, from time to time He allowed them to see with their eyes the promised Savior."[70]

It is also interesting to note that most of the Christophanies occur in the first five books of the Old Testament (prior to the Law being given and sacrifices instituted).

There are several passages that allude to the active, "physical" presence of God after the Exodus and through the wilderness wandering.

Leviticus 26:12- *[12] I will also **walk** among you and be your God, and you shall be My people.*

---

[69] Hebrews 11:27, NASB.
[70] Michael P. V. Barrett, *Beginning at Moses: A Guide to Finding Christ in the Old Testament* (Greenville: Ambassador-Emerald International, 1999), 163.

Deuteronomy 23:14- *¹⁴ Since the Lord your God walks in the midst of your camp to deliver you and to defeat your enemies before you, therefore your camp must be holy; and He must not see anything indecent among you or He will turn away from you.*

Christophanies in the Old Testament

The Lord Appeared (exact phrase in Scripture)

Genesis 12:7 - to Abram upon promising the land

Genesis 17:1 - to Abraham

Genesis 18:1 - to Abraham at the oaks of Mamre

Genesis 26:2 - to Isaac warning him not to go to Egypt

Genesis 26:24 - to Isaac promising He will multiply his descendants

Deuteronomy 31:15 - to Moses prior to his death

1 Samuel- 3:21 - to Samuel at Shiloh

2 Chronicles 7:12 - to Solomon affirming the building of the Temple

Jeremiah 31:3 - to Jeremiah promising restoration

The Lord Came Down (exact phrase in Scripture)

Genesis 11:5 - at the building of the Tower of Babel

Exodus 19:18, 20 - with Moses on Mt. Sinai

Numbers 11:25 - Put the Spirit on 70 elders

Numbers 12:5, 8 - to Moses, Aaron and Miriam at the tent of meeting

Exodus 34:5 - to Moses upon giving him the stone tablets of the Law

The Lord Stood (exact phrase in Scripture)

Genesis 28:13 - Jacob's dream of a ladder (could be a vision)

Exodus 17:6 - on the Rock at Horeb

Numbers 20:11 - on the Rock at Horeb (same as Exodus 17:6)*

Walked with God (exact phrase in Scripture)

Genesis 5:22, 24 - Enoch walked with God

Genesis 6:9 - Noah walked with God

Other Christophanies

Genesis 3:8 - walking with Adam and Eve in the garden

Genesis 15 - Christ walks through the pieces of the animals while cutting covenant with Abraham

Genesis 32 - Jacob wrestles with Christ**

Exodus 4:24 - the Lord "met" Moses and sought to put him to death

Exodus 24:9-11 - Moses, Aaron, Nadab, Abihu and the 70 elders see the God of Israel on the mountain

Joshua 5:13-15 - to Joshua as the Captain of The Host of the Lord

Jeremiah 1:4-10 - The Word of the Lord comes to Jeremiah (this same phrase is used in many other Old Testament passages). However, here, the Lord "stretched out His hand and touched" Jeremiah's mouth.[71]

Daniel 3:23-25 - as the fourth man in the fiery furnace who looked like a son of the gods

*See 1 Corinthians 10:4 for The Apostle Paul's interpretation of this appearance

**See Hosea 12:3-5

There are many more passages in Scripture that could be Christophanies. I only listed the exact phrases found in Scripture.

In the following chapters, I will chronicle the pre-incarnate appearances of Christ in the Old Testament one by one. These will only be actual pre-incarnate appearances, not typology, prophecy, or allusions to Christ. Nor will I include the appearances of Christ in dreams and visions. Thus, this list presents a very narrow focus.

---

[71] Jeremiah 1:9, NASB.

Chapter Nine

Christ in the Beginning

(Genesis 1-11)

Genesis 1:1

"In the beginning God created the heavens and the earth."

I have already shown that, according to John 1:1, The Word (Christ) was in the beginning with God. Therefore, it is difficult for me to imagine the very act of Creation without the presence of Christ. To say that Christ's presence during Creation was not a Christophany, or appearance of Christ, although particularly accurate according to the text, seems completely unfounded in truth.

In verse 3 of John 1, the Bible affirms Christ's role in creation. "All things came into being by Him, and apart from Him nothing came into being that has come into being."[72]

Prior to the beginning of the people of God as a nation under Abraham, God, in the person of Christ appeared to His creation on several occasions.

---

[72] Genesis 1:3, NASB

Genesis 3:8 (#1)

8 They heard the sound of the Lord God walking in the garden in the cool of the day, and the man and his wife hid themselves from the presence of the Lord God among the trees of the garden.

The crown of God's creation was man and woman, fashioned in the image of Himself. According to this verse, man enjoyed intimate fellowship with God in the person of the pre-incarnate Christ.

As discussed in Chapter four, the Aramaic word, memra, is used in the Jewish Targums to identify the personification of God as active in the Old Testament. Jonathan Bernis reminds us, "Memra, according to the Jewish Encyclopedia, means "The Word."[73] We learned that Genesis 3:8 could be read as, "They heard the voice of the Memra of the Lord God walking in the Garden."[74] Notice that the Hebrew for our English word "sound" in the NASB is translated as "voice."

Furthermore, the most important word in the whole verse regarding an appearance of the pre-incarnate Christ may be the word "walking." I contend, according to my fundamental

---

[73] Bernis, Jonathan. "Finding Jesus in the Old Testament" www.charismamag.com Accessed April 19, 2016. http://www.charismamag.com/spirit/bible-study/15023-finding-jesus-in-the-old-testament
[74] Read, W.E.. "Christ The Logos-The Word of God" www.ministrymagazine.org Accessed June 30, 2016. https://www.ministrymagazine.org/archive/1958/08/christ-the-logos-the-word-of-god

assertion, that any personification of God in the Old Testament should be identified with the pre-incarnate Christ.

Genesis 5:22, 24 (#2)

22 Then Enoch walked with God three hundred years after he became the father of Methuselah, and he had other sons and daughters. 24 Enoch walked with God; and he was not, for God took him.

This passage falls in a lengthy list of ten generations from Adam to Noah. Apparently, the list represents a decline of the moral fabric of the people populating planet earth given that during the time of the last man in the list, God judges the earth with a flood.

Chuck Missler shares a riddle concerning Enoch. "Here is a question to ask your Biblically literate friends: If Methuselah was the oldest man in the Bible, how could he die before his father?"[75] The answer is that Enoch never really died, as best we can discern. He walked with God and he was not.[76] Given the use of a Hebrew word for "walk" which means exactly that, we must conclude (as in Genesis 3) that this was a pre-incarnate appearance of Christ.

Interestingly enough, a study of the root word meanings of the names of these ten generations in Genesis 5 yields an incredible insight. Chuck Missler goes into great detail to explain the meanings of the root words in his book, <u>Hidden Treasures in the Biblical Text</u>. Let me just give you the summary of the meanings of the ten generations from Adam to Noah.

---

[75] Missler, Chuck. "Hidden Treasures in the Biblical Text." Coeur d'Alene: Koinonia House. Kindle Edition. 128.
[76] Genesis 5:24, NASB

Hebrew	English
Adam	Man
Seth	Appointed
Enosh	Mortal
Kenan	Sorrow
Mahalalel	The Blessed God
Jared	Shall Come Down
Enoch	Teaching
Methuselah	His Death Shall Bring
Lamech	Despairing
Noah	Rest

Missler summarizes by writing, "Man (is) appointed mortal sorrow; (but) the Blessed God shall come down teaching (that) His death shall bring (the) despairing rest." Here is a summary of God's plan of redemption, hidden here within a genealogy in Genesis! "[77] While this is not a pre-incarnate appearance of Christ, it was too remarkable not to share.

Genesis 6:9 (#3)

9 These are the records of the generations of Noah. Noah was a righteous man, blameless in his time; Noah walked with God.

In much the same way that I believe Enoch walked with God, we find in the very next chapter that Noah walked with the pre-incarnate Christ as well.

---

[77] Missler, Chuck. "Hidden Treasures in the Biblical Text." Coeur d'Alene: Koinonia House. Kindle Edition. Kindle Locations 223-225.

Genesis 11:5 (#4)

5 The Lord came down to see the city and the tower which the sons of men had built.

This passage is the first time the language is used that the Lord "came down." As discussed in chapter eight, this represents, in my opinion, a Chistophany, or pre-incarnate appearance of Christ.

In addition, a few verses later, the Scripture says, "Come, let Us go down and there confuse their language."[78] The use of the plural form, "Us," in the language lends further support to the Trinity or Godhead. Which, points toward the Son of God, the pre-incarnate Christ being present.

Later, God scatters the people across the face of the earth.[79] To this point, God has created man, pursued a relationship with him, judged his disobedience to the point of flooding the earth and scattered them across the face of the earth. God is pursuing a relationship with His people, a relationship that is real and personal.

---

[78] Genesis 11:7, NASB
[79] Genesis 11:8, NASB

John M. Burris

Chapter Ten

Christ Appears to Abraham

(Genesis 12-22)

God, in His wisdom, chooses a man named Abram to become the patriarch of a nation that God would make into His special people.[80]

Genesis 12:4-9 (#5)

*4 So Abram went forth as the Lord had spoken to him; and Lot went with him. Now Abram was seventy-five years old when he departed from Haran. 5 Abram took Sarai his wife and Lot his nephew, and all their possessions which they had accumulated, and the persons which they had acquired in Haran, and they set out for the land of Canaan; thus they came to the land of Canaan. 6 Abram passed through the land as far as the site of Shechem, to the oak of Moreh. Now the Canaanite was then in the land. 7 The Lord **appeared** to Abram and said, "To your descendants I will give this land." So he built an altar there to the Lord who had appeared to him. 8 Then he proceeded from there to the mountain on the east of Bethel, and pitched his tent, with Bethel on the west and Ai on the east; and there he built an altar to the Lord and called upon the name of the Lord. 9 Abram journeyed on, continuing toward the Negev.*

---

[80] Genesis 12:1-3, NASB

Abram responded to God's invitation to follow Him with obedience and set out for the land that God would show him.

The map below shows the route that Abram is believed to have taken. Notice that it takes him to a land that was occupied by the people of Caanan, descendants of Noah's son Ham.

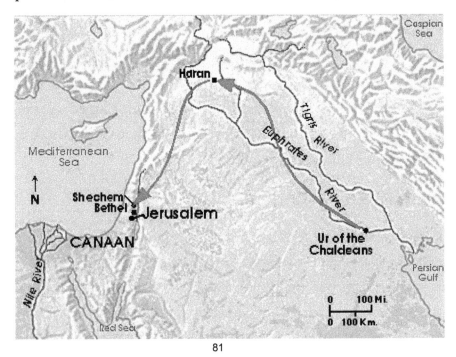

81

What is striking to me is the distance Abram would have traveled had he heard a voice or sensed that God was calling him. It is much more likely that Abram left and followed after a personal encounter with God in the person of Christ.

Notice also the significance of verse 7, "And the Lord **appeared** to Abram and **said**..." Could this be what Jesus was referring to in

81 Map of Abraham's Travels. Digital image. Abraham. Accessed July 13, 2016. http://www.bible-archaeology.info/abraham.htm

John 8:56 when He said, "Your Father Abraham rejoiced to see My day, and he saw it and was glad."?

I believe Abraham saw Jesus' Day (a generic sense of time in the Greek) on multiple occasions. The first of which is here in the Genesis 12 passage.

The next appearance of Jesus in the Old Testament occurs in Genesis chapter 15. This will be perhaps the most significant meeting between the pre-incarnate Christ and Abraham.

Genesis 15:1-18 (#6)

v.1- "The word of the Lord came to Abram"- As discussed in chapter 4, when the phrase, "the word of the Lord came to" is used, some scholars believe that to mean the presence of the pre-incarnate Christ.

Abram responds in **verse 2** by saying, "O Lord God"

According to **verse 5**, this is not just a voice speaking from heaven, "And He took him outside"

Abram was concerned that he had no heir to carry out the promise God had made to him. If all of the earth would be blessed through his descendants, and he had none, how was God's promise going to be fulfilled? (Gen. 12:2-3)

As Christ then, takes him outside, He reassures Abram of the promise. (v.5)

Verse 6 is the statement of Abram's faith that Paul makes much of in the New Testament as the basis of righteousness.[82]

"Then he **believed in** the Lord; and **He** reckoned it to him as righteousness."

The Hebrew word that is translated for us as "believed in" is an important word. It is not just an intellectual affirmation. Abram is not just saying that he knows about God. He is communicating trust.

The Hebrew word, *aman*, can mean to establish, to be firm, communicating faithfulness and trustworthiness.

Vine's Dictionary says of this word, "It was not primarily in God's words that he believed, but in God Himself...In other words, Abram came to experience a personal relationship to God rather than an impersonal relationship with His promises."[83]

The next thing The Lord does with Abram is enter into a covenant with him.

Abram brings animals for a sacrifice, cuts them in two pieces and lays them on the ground across from each other creating a path in between the pieces. (v.10)

v.13- and **God** said to Abram... He reaffirms the covenant promise of Abram having descendants.

---

[82] Romans 4, NASB

[83] W.E. Vine, Merrill F. Unger, William White Jr., Vine's Complete Expository Dictionary of Old and New Testament Words (Nashville: Thomas Nelson Publishers, 1985), 16.

v.17- there appeared a smoking oven, or furnace as in the KJV. This is always used in the Old Testament as a symbol of God's avenging presence. The fact that it is smoking is reminiscent of the pillar of smoke that guided the Israelites on their flight from Egypt.

A flaming torch or a burning lamp (KJV)- The Hebrew word for flaming is used often as a symbol for God (Exodus 3:2, 13:21-22, 19:18, Deut. 4:11). This word was also used to describe the burning of the sacrifices on the brazen altar.

Torch or lamp- used mainly of fiery light. Also depicts bright flashes of lightning or the eyes of a divine being in Daniel 10:6, Exodus 20:18-21.

v.18- On that day the Lord made a covenant with Abram- The word in Hebrew for made is "to cut." This would be the explanation for cutting the animals in two pieces. The practice was for the parties in the covenant to walk between the pieces to make the covenant, a formal binding agreement.

Who was Abram cutting covenant with? He was entering into covenant with God in the person of Christ. In my opinion, this was what Jesus was referring to when He said, "Abraham rejoiced to see My day."

In essence, God made a covenant with Himself. This indicates not only the Trinity, but also the fact that God's plan for man is initiated and carried out by Him apart from human involvement. God's covenant would not depend on man's ability to keep that covenant.

The covenant making, covenant-keeping God has met with Abram to establish the joy of a relationship and begin a work in him that will result in all the people of the earth being blessed.

Genesis 16:7-11 (#7)

7 Now the angel of the Lord found her by a spring of water in the wilderness, by the spring on the way to Shur. 8 He said, "Hagar, Sarai's maid, where have you come from and where are you going?" And she said, "I am fleeing from the presence of my mistress Sarai." 9 Then the angel of the Lord said to her, "Return to your mistress, and submit yourself to her authority." 10 Moreover, the angel of the Lord said to her, "I will greatly multiply your descendants so that they will be too many to count." 11 The angel of the Lord said to her further,

"Behold, you are with child,

And you will bear a son;

And you shall call his name Ishmael,

Because the Lord has given heed to your affliction.

Part of the covenant which God made with Abram was to make him into a great nation. For Abram and his wife Sarai, this would seem to be a difficult promise to keep given the fact that they are already old and have no children. So, Sarai concocted a plan to begin the process of making a nation through her own plan. She would allow Abram to father a child through her Egyptian maid, Hagar. This would give Abram the descendent he would need to begin to build a nation. Sarai's actions are not much different than our actions when we decide the direction for our lives rather than trusting God's direction.

Abram does indeed father a child through Hagar. As a result, Sarai despised the pregnant Hagar and treated her harshly.[84] This caused Hagar to flee from Sarai and Abram.

v.7- This is the first mention in Scripture of "the angel of the Lord." We have already discussed in chapter 7 that most scholars believe that the angel of the Lord is the pre-incarnate Christ.

v.9- Notice that the angel of the Lord speaks to Hagar.

v.10- In this verse the angel of the Lord makes a promise to Hagar that only God can fulfill. This sets the angel of the Lord apart from any human or ordinary angel who would not be able to deliver on this promise.

v.11- Finally, the angel of the Lord reveals to Hagar what will come of the child she is carrying.

Genesis 17:1 (#8)

17 Now when Abram was ninety-nine years old, the Lord appeared to Abram and said to him,

"I am God Almighty;

Walk before Me, and be blameless.

Here, the Lord appeared to Abram and said "I am God Almighty." He then went on to reaffirm His covenant with Abram (Exalted Father) and change his name to Abraham (Father of many nations). By the way, this was after a thirteen-year period during

---

[84] Genesis 16:6, NASB

which the only descendant was one of the sinful union between Abram and Hagar.

The Lord also promises a child to be born to Abraham and Sarah in their old age.[85] It will be through this child, Isaac, that God establishes the nation of Israel and fulfills His covenant promise.

Genesis 18:1 (#9)

18 Now the Lord appeared to him by the oaks of Mamre, while he was sitting at the tent door in the heat of the day.

v.1- the Lord **appeared** to him

v.2- three men were standing opposite him and he **bowed himself** to the earth

v.13- the Lord **said** to Abraham

v.15- Sarah was **afraid**

v.19- The Lord reaffirms His promise and plan for Abraham

v.22- the men turned away while Abraham was still standing before the Lord

v.33- as soon as He had finished speaking, the Lord **departed**

Genesis 21:17 (#10)

17 God heard the lad crying; and the angel of God called to Hagar from heaven and said to her, "What is the matter with you, Hagar? Do not fear, for God has heard the voice of the lad where he is.

---

[85] Genesis 17:19, NASB

Here we find the angel of God (Christ) speaking to Hagar from Heaven. Even though He is not appearing, He is still speaking to Hagar.

Genesis 22:11,15 (#11)

11 But the angel of the Lord called to him from heaven and said, "Abraham, Abraham!" And he said, "Here I am." 15 Then the angel of the Lord called to Abraham a second time from heaven,

In Chapter 22 of Genesis, we find one of the most profound examples of typology in the Bible. Simply put, a "type" is a person or thing in the Old Testament that is a foreshadowing of someone or something in the New Testament.

V.1 **God tested Abraham-** You might think this action of God is cruel or even unnecessary. If God knows all things, why would he need to test Abraham? Didn't he know how he would respond? Yes, but Abraham didn't know! When God tested His people in the Old Testament, it always had to do with their willingness to obey or surrender. God's testing is not for God to learn something new. He knows all things. The testing is for us, to teach us something about God and our relationship with Him.

V.2 **Your only son-** I believe this is in reference to Abraham's only son of the promise. Abraham had Ishmael with Hagar, but it was Isaac who was the son that God had promised to Abraham. **Hebrews 11:17** refers to Isaac as Abraham's only begotten son.

V.2 **Land of Moriah-** Abraham lived in Beersheba, 40 miles from the region of Moriah. By the way, Moriah means "chosen by Jehovah." A burnt offering was an offering that was to indicate devotion, commitment, and complete surrender to God.

V.4   **Saw the place from a distance-** This would indicate that Moriah was likely the highest peak.

Region of Moriah- 3 low mountains, olives (East), Zion (West), Moriah (middle). Mt. Moriah has a series of ridges.

At 600 meters above sea level is the town of Salem. This city becomes Ophel, city of David and eventually Jerusalem.

At 741 meters above sea level there is a Saddle Point. It was at this spot that Araunah owned a threshing floor. This would become the sight of Solomon's Temple, the dwelling place of God. (2 Chronicles 3:1). This is also fulfillment of the prophecy back in Genesis 10 that God would dwell in the tents of Shem.

At 777 meters above sea level is the peak. This location is north of Temple Mount, later to be known as Golgotha, the place of the skull where Jesus was crucified for our sin. Map below:

http://www.generationword.com/jerusalem101/1-biblical-jerusalem.html

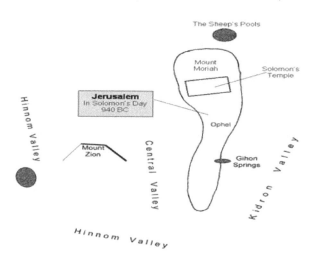

On the third day- Notice the journey took three days. In essence, Isaac was "dead" to Abraham for those three days.

V.5   **We will worship __and__ return to you**. See here Abraham's faith. Hebrews 11:19 says, "Abraham reasoned that God could raise the dead." Abraham believed that God would raise Isaac from the dead. By the way, as far as we know the dead had never been raised before.

This would not be the last time that worship would take place on this mount. Remember, it would be this very piece of property that King David would purchase from Araunah. (2 Samuel 24:24-25)

Neither would this be the first act of worship on this mount. In the account of Abram and Melchizedek in Genesis 14, Melchizedek is described as the King of Salem. That would be the King of Jerusalem. He would have been a Caananite King who clearly according to the text, worshiped Jehovah God. This is further evidence that the Caananites would have been exposed to the truth of God, and therefore accountable, long before the days when Joshua would enter the Promised Land with the instructions to eradicate those who dwelt in the land.

V.6   **Laid the wood on Isaac**- Just as the cross was laid on Christ to walk up that same hill, Isaac carried the wood for his own sacrificial altar.

V.7   Isaac becomes curious as to what is going to be sacrificed.

V.8   Notice Abraham's response. God will provide *himself* the lamb. The original word in Hebrew for provide is "to see" and the flow in the Hebrew is, "God will see Himself a Lamb." The word for provide is used in other passages of scripture as behold or consider.

V.9   **Bound his son Isaac and laid him on the altar-** The text treats this very routinely. Our Sunday school minds have always made Isaac a small boy. The word lad in verse 5 means "young man," one old enough to serve in battle or as a personal private force. In fact, according to several chronological resources, Isaac was around 33 years old.

V.10-12 Burnt offering- In Leviticus 1:4 the procedure requires first to put the hand on the head of the sacrifice. This symbolized belonging or identification with the sacrifice. Notice in Gen. 22:10-12, Abraham has just stretched out his hand for the knife, and the first instructions of the angel of the Lord in verse 12 are, "do not stretch out your hand against the lad." The KJV says, "lay not your hand upon the lad."

V.10   We have this idea that God waited until the last second before he stopped Abraham. But God stopped him right where he wanted to stop him. Yes, Isaac was Abraham's son. But, he was only on loan from God. You see, those of us with children, though we love them more than anything, we should know they belong to God.

V.11   **Angel of the Lord-** As we have seen, many scholars agree that the reference to the Angel of the Lord in the OT is actually the pre-incarnate Christ! I believe he heard this voice before!

V.13   God had indeed provided a ram for a proper sacrifice. Notice the text says Abraham offered him up in the place of his son. (1 Peter 2:24)

V.14-18 Here Abraham hears that familiar voice. He hears the same covenant promise that God will bring to fulfillment. God had been faithful once to provide a son of promise in the first place. Now Abraham's faith had been tested again and God's faithfulness proved sufficient.

V.19 Abraham returned to his young men. The text does not mention Isaac at all. In fact, Isaac is not mentioned again until he is united with his bride Rebekah in chapter 24. Isaac, who is the "type" of Christ, leaves the scene until he is united with His bride. In the same way, Jesus, having accomplished the purpose of salvation, returns to Heaven until He comes again for His bride, the Church.

In addition, it is Abraham's servant, Eliezer, which means "comforter", who is given charge to gather the bride for Isaac. The Holy Spirit, or as Jesus refers to Him, The Comforter, unites us to Christ. (1 John 4:13)

Frank Viola, in his book, <u>Jesus Now</u>, writes, "The Holy Spirit unites us to Jesus Christ and to His body. The Spirit reveals Christ to us, gives us His life, and makes Christ alive in us. The Spirit takes the experiences of Jesus . . . His incarnation, ministry, crucifixion, resurrection, and ascension . . . and brings them into our own experience. Because of the Holy Spirit, the history of Jesus Christ becomes our story and experience."[86]

Now see how this ties together in regard to Christ...

- God took His only son

- To a place chosen by Jehovah

- To the very same peak of the very same mountain

- God beheld Himself, (His Son) as the lamb of God that would take away the sins of the world

---

[86] http://wineskins.org/2014/05/05/the-spirit-of-jesus/

- And He bound Him with our sins and laid Him on the cross-shaped altar

- But this time the living sacrifice was not spared. But, instead, God allowed the nails to pierce His hands and feet.

Not only is Isaac a "type" for Christ foreshadowing His journey to the cross, but The Angel of the Lord, who is Christ Himself, called to Abraham on Mount Moriah.

Chapter Eleven

Christ Appears to Isaac and Jacob

(Genesis 26-32)

Interestingly, Isaac is never recorded as having come down the mountain with Abraham. In fact, we do not see Isaac's name in Scripture until two chapters later when he is united with his bride Rebekah. Even more interesting is that it is Abraham's servant, Eliezer, whose name means "God of Help," who is the one charged with bringing the two together.

As you can see, the typology is rich in meaning. Isaac, a type of Christ, after having been, in effect, "sacrificed" on the same mountain as Christ would be crucified and "resurrected" by the intervention of the Angel of the Lord. Furthermore, Isaac is absent from the text until he is united with his bride (a type of the church), who are brought together by Eliezer, the servant or helper (a type of The Holy Spirit). One is only left to marvel at the precise detail of God's dealings with His people. These details are beyond being contrived. God's perfect wisdom is on display in His Word.

God continues to affirm His covenant with Abraham even after his death through his descendants, particularly Isaac and Jacob. Here in Genesis 26, Scripture says that God "appeared" to Isaac on two different occasions. The Hebrew word translated "appeared" in the NASB has a relatively simple meaning, *to see.*

Christ Appears to Isaac

Genesis 26:2 (#12)

*2 The Lord **appeared** to him and said, "Do not go down to Egypt; stay in the land of which I shall tell you.*

Verse 1 of the passage indicates that the land was experiencing a famine. Apparently, the famine was serious enough for Isaac to consider going to Egypt. The Lord appeared to him and urged him not to go to Egypt. Then, the Lord reaffirmed the covenant He had made with Isaac's father Abraham.

3 Sojourn in this land and I will be with you and bless you, for to you and to your descendants I will give all these lands, and I will establish the oath which I swore to your father Abraham. 4 I will multiply your descendants as the stars of heaven, and will give your descendants all these lands; and by your descendants all the nations of the earth shall be blessed; 5 because Abraham obeyed Me and kept My charge, My commandments, My statutes and My laws."[87]

Isaac then encountered great difficulty in acquiring water. Through the actions of the Philistines and the herdsmen of Gerar, Isaac had to move several times in order to find a suitable source for water. Yet again, the Lord appeared to him and assured Isaac of His promises and covenant.

Genesis 26:24 (#13)

*24 The Lord **appeared** to him the same night and said,*

---

[87] Genesis 26:3-5, NASB

"I am the God of your father Abraham;

Do not fear, for I am with you.

I will bless you, and multiply your descendants,

For the sake of My servant Abraham."

Notice that the Lord did not specifically address the issue of food or water in each of the circumstances that concerned Isaac. The Lord always pointed back to the covenant as a reminder of His constant provision, protection and presence. It seems to me that the very presence of God in the form of the pre-incarnate Christ would supersede any apparent lack of food or water.

Christ Appears to Jacob

Genesis 28:12-13 (#14)

[12] *He had a dream, and behold, a ladder was set on the earth with its top reaching to heaven; and behold, the angels of God were ascending and descending on it.* [13] *And behold,* **the Lord stood** *above it and said, "I am the Lord, the God of your father Abraham and the God of Isaac; the land on which you lie, I will give it to you and to your descendants.*

While some would argue that this is merely a dream and does not actually constitute an appearance of Christ, Jacob's response to the dream indicates more of a reality than any normal dream.

The Hebrew word for stood is a verb meaning, "to station...to take a stand. Abraham's servant stationed himself beside the well to find a wife for Isaac."[88]

---

[88] The Complete Word Study Dictionary: Old Testament, 747.

Notice in verse 16 that, as Jacob awakens from the vision, he declares, "Surely the Lord is in this place, and I did not know it." Furthermore, he went on, "And he was afraid and said, 'How awesome is this place! This is none other than the house of God, and this is the gate of Heaven.'"[89] Jacob then names the place of the vision, Bethel, which means "House of God."

The most convincing argument that this was indeed a Christophany and not merely a dream stems from Jacob himself. In Genesis 48, Jacob is near the end of his life and he gathers Joseph and his sons, Ephraim and Manasseh, to his side.

Genesis 48:3

*³ Then Jacob said to Joseph, "**God Almighty appeared to me at Luz** in the land of Canaan and blessed me,*

I believe this is a direct reference back to the events of Genesis 28 and therefore, a pre-incarnate appearance of Christ. In fact, Genesis 28:19 states, "And he called the name of that place Bethel, however, previously the name of the city had been Luz."[90]

Genesis 31:11-13 (#15)

11 Then the angel of God said to me in the dream, 'Jacob,' and I said, 'Here I am.'12 He said, 'Lift up now your eyes and see that all the male goats which are mating are striped, speckled, and mottled; for I have seen all that Laban has been doing to you. 13 I am the God of Bethel, where

---

[89] Genesis 28:17, NASB.
[90] Genesis 28:19, NASB.

you anointed a pillar, where you made a vow to Me; now arise, leave this land, and return to the land of your birth.'"

The Lord instructs Jacob to leave the land of Laban. For quite some time, Laban has tried to cheat Jacob out of wages that were due him. Apparently, there were several possible implications with Jacob leaving, most notably the fact that Laban was his father-in-law.

If you remember, there was a mention of "the angel of the Lord" in Genesis chapter 16. Notice that this angel of the God here in Genesis 31 identifies Himself as God. In fact, He points back to the vision that Jacob had in chapter 28 by referring to the place that Jacob had named Bethel.

I believe that the one Jacob hears speaking to him in a dream, as well as the one Hagar spoke with in Genesis 16 is none other than Christ, the Son of God.

Jacob has another important encounter in Genesis 32. Here Jacob finds himself between the fear of what lies ahead (an encounter with Esau) and the realization that he cannot go back to the land of Laban.

In verse 1, we see the phrase "the angels of God." This same phrase is used in Genesis 28 in the vision of the ladder where the angels of God were ascending and descending.[91] Immediately, Jacob identifies the place he has come upon as "God's camp" or "God's company." He then named the place *Mahanaim*, which means, "two camps."[92] This is an interesting word in the Hebrew.

---

[91] Genesis 28:12, NASB
[92] Genesis 32:2, NASB

At first glance, the *–im* ending, indicates a plural noun. Upon further investigation, however, it actually indicates the rather rare dual form. There is much debate as to the exact nature of the two camps to which Jacob refers. Most scholars take the meaning to be one camp being the heavenly camp of the angels of God and the other being Jacobs rather significant earthly camp. Nevertheless, there are a lot of "twos" that accompany Jacob's story through Genesis.

- Two nations at war within Rebekah (Genesis 25:23)

- Two peoples separated from Rebekah's body (Genesis 25:23)

- Twins in Rebekah's womb, Jacob and Esau (Genesis 25:24)

- Two wives of Jacob, Leah and Rachel (Genesis 29)

- Two camps as the name of the place where Jacob met the angels of God (Genesis 32:1-2)

- Two camps made from all of Jacob's people and possessions (Genesis 32:7)

Jacob now finds himself in full fear of facing Esau, whom he had talked out of his birthright and tricked out of Isaac's blessing. Surely the retaliation of Esau would be fierce when they meet again.

After sending ahead of him all that he owns and eventually his wives, maidens and children, Jacob is left alone to stew in his fear. It is in this moment that he has an encounter with the pre-incarnate Christ.

Genesis 32:24-31 (#16)

²⁴ Then Jacob was left alone, and a man wrestled with him until daybreak. ²⁵ When he saw that he had not prevailed against him, he touched the socket of his thigh; so the socket of Jacob's thigh was dislocated while he wrestled with him. ²⁶ Then he said, "Let me go, for the dawn is breaking." But he said, "I will not let you go unless you bless me." ²⁷ So he said to him, "What is your name?" And he said, "Jacob." ²⁸ He said, "Your name shall no longer be Jacob, but Israel; for you have striven with God and with men and have prevailed." ²⁹ Then Jacob asked him and said, "Please tell me your name." But he said, "Why is it that you ask my name?" And he blessed him there. ³⁰ So Jacob named the place Peniel, for he said, "I have seen God face to face, yet my life has been preserved." ³¹ Now the sun rose upon him just as he crossed over Penuel, and he was limping on his thigh.

- A man wrestled with Jacob (v.24)

- The man was physical because he touched Jacob's hip (v.24)

- Jacob understood the special nature of the man because he wanted his blessing (v.26)

- The man identifies Himself to Jacob through changing his name from Jacob to Israel (God rules) (v.28)

- Jacob named the site of the struggle Peniel (the face of God), because he realized he had been wrestling with God (v.30)

Hosea 12:3-5 gives us further insight into this encounter.

³ In the womb he took his brother by the heel,

And in his maturity, he contended with God.

⁴ Yes, he wrestled with the angel and prevailed;

He wept and sought His favor.

He found Him at Bethel

And there He spoke with us,

⁵ Even the Lord, the God of hosts,

The Lord is His name.

This passage makes it clear that this was no mere man that wrestled with Jacob. It was indeed the Lord, the God of hosts.

But, there is one more important aspect of this encounter that we must understand. In Genesis 32:27, the Lord asks Jacob what seems to be a very strange question. The question itself is not strange, but the fact that the Lord would even need to ask it is the strange part. We have already established that this is Christ in His pre-incarnate form, the omniscient second person of the Trinity. He asks Jacob, "What is your name?" Of course, He knows who He is wrestling with. But, as Ravi Zacharias so beautifully points out, the last time Jacob was asked this question it was by his father and his answer was to lie and steal the blessing that belonged to Esau.[93]

This almost seems to be a chilling encounter. In the throes of wrestling with God Himself, Jacob is confronted with not only his past deceit but the realization that his path forward depends on how he answers the question. Perhaps in that moment, he realized that he could not hide from the one who knows all things.

---

[93] http://rzim.org/just-a-thought-broadcasts/what-is-your-name/

Hebrews 4:13 says, *"And there is no creature hidden from His sight, but all things are open and laid bare to the eyes of Him with whom we have to do."* The Greek word for "laid bare" in that verse is a word that means, "the bending back of the neck of wrestlers by their opponent."[94] It is the Greek word that yields our English word trachea, referring to the throat. Here in a wrestling grip of the one who formed him in Rebekah's womb, Jacob may have found that he was completely exposed. There was no more hiding.

Furthermore, the verse indicates in its original language that we all are exposed, or laid bare, before the eyes of Him with whom we have to do. Another translation reads, before the eyes of Him to whom we must give account.[95] The actual Greek word in the original text for the word "do" or "account" is actually the Greek word *Logos*, which we determined in Chapter 4 to be the Word of God, Jesus Christ. So, Jacob was totally exposed and face to face with Christ.

The Lord's response was to tell Jacob that he will no longer be called by the name Jacob, which meant "grasps the heel" pointing to his first activity after emerging form Rebekah's womb. He would now be called Israel, which means "God rules." From this point forward, the name Israel would remind him of this moment when, being gripped by Majesty, he came face to face with God and himself.

How is it that Israel, having tricked his brother out of his birthright and deceived his father out of his blessing would become the one from whom the very people of God would be established,

[94] The Complete Word Study Dictionary: New Testament, 1393.
[95] Hebrews 4:13, NIV

including the Messiah?   The straightforward answer is…God determined that to be so. We cannot know fully the mind and plan of Almighty God. But, it does give hope to sinners like me who come face to face with Majesty and must acknowledge our need for Him. We find that He meets us with grace and changes our name as well to sons and daughters of the King.

[17] *Therefore if anyone is in Christ, he is a new creature; the old things passed away; behold, new things have come.*[96]

---

[96] 2 Corinthians 5:17, NASB

Chapter Twelve

Christ in the Exodus

(Exodus)

Jacob (Israel) would go on to father the twelve children who would become the leaders of the twelve tribes that would become the nation of Israel. Many years later a man named Moses would be born. Moses was the great great grandson of Jacob. Moses was born into a time that saw the Israelites facing harsh treatment at the hands of Egypt, a nation that did not recognize Jehovah as God.

The Israelites people were in slavery to the Egyptians. At the age of 80, Moses had an encounter that would change his life and the future of the Hebrew people.

Exodus 1

In this chapter, while there does not seem to be a spoken word by God or a visible manifestation, there does seem to be the assembling of a nation. The number of the Hebrews in Egypt goes from 70 just before Joseph died to now at the time of Moses' birth, perhaps a million or more. This rapid birth rate is described here in chapter one.

There is an interesting Hebrew word use in verse 21 that implies that God "made" households for the midwives of the Hebrew people. The Hebrew word for "made", or "established" as in the NASB, is one that is used in many OT references to the physical act of building or making something. If nothing else, this does seem to be personification.

Exodus 2

When the leadership changed in Egypt, the mistreatment of the Hebrew people must have increased to the point of desperation. So much so that they began to cry out to God.

Four words are used to describe God's response to their cries in verse 24-25.

God heard

God remembered

God saw

God took notice (Hebrew-to know experientially and relationally)

Exodus 3:1-22 (#17)

Verse 2 states that "the angel of the Lord" appeared to Moses amid a burning bush. If you are like me, most of your visual imagery concerning this event is Moses approaching a bush in the middle of the desert that is on fire but is not burning up. And then, Moses proceeds to have a talk with the voice of God that is echoing from the bush.

The presence of the angel of the Lord here in this passage should change that visual imagery.

Justin Martyr declared, "Our Christ conversed with Moses out of the bush, in the appearance of fire. And Moses received great strength from Christ, who spake to him in the appearance of fire."[97]

Irenaeus wrote, "The Scripture is full of the Son of God's appearing: sometimes to talk and eat with Abraham, at other times to instruct Noah about the measures of the ark; at another time to seek Adam; at another time to bring down judgment upon Sodom; then again, to direct Jacob in the way; and again, to converse with Moses out of the bush."[98]

Henry Law, in his book, Gleanings from the Book of Life, wrote, "We here learn that Jesus is "the Angel of the Lord." The voice announced, "I am God," and the appearance exhibited a human form. Who can be both God and man but Jesus? The Father never appeared as man. The Holy Spirit never thus condescended. But the blessed Jesus, anticipating the time when earth should claim Him as its child, not infrequently assumed our form. Therefore, without hesitation, we receive "the Angel of the Lord" as Jesus the incarnate God."[99]

Notice that the same word is used here as in the account of Abraham and the covenant of God (*flaming* in Genesis 15:17 the same as *fire* in Exodus 3:2). We have already seen that Christ was

[97] Precept Austin. "Who is The Angel of The Lord?" www.preceptaustin.org Accessed June 26, 2016.
http://www.preceptaustin.org/angel_of_the_lord.htm
[98] Precept Austin. "Who is The Angel of The Lord?" www.preceptaustin.org Accessed June 26, 2016.
http://www.preceptaustin.org/angel_of_the_lord.htm
[99] Precept Austin. "Who is The Angel of The Lord?" www.preceptaustin.org Accessed June 26, 2016.
http://www.preceptaustin.org/angel_of_the_lord.htm

the one who passed between the pieces of the sacrifice and now the same language is used to describe what Moses saw in the bush.

Two New Testament passages also affirm this idea that Moses saw more than just a bush on fire.

Acts 7: 30, 35, 38

30 "After forty years had passed, an angel appeared to him in the wilderness of Mount Sinai, in the flame of a burning thorn bush...35 "This Moses whom they disowned, saying, 'Who made you a ruler and a judge?' is the one whom God sent to be both a ruler and a deliverer with the help of the angel who appeared to him in the thorn bush...38 This is the one who was in the congregation in the wilderness together with the angel who was speaking to him on Mount Sinai, and who was with our fathers; and he received living oracles to pass on to you.

These verses all reference an angel that appeared to Moses (v.30), helped Moses (v.35) and spoke to Moses (v.38).

Hebrews 11:24-27

*24 By faith Moses, when he had grown up, refused to be called the son of Pharaoh's daughter, 25 choosing rather to endure ill-treatment with the people of God than to enjoy the passing pleasures of sin, 26 considering the reproach of Christ greater riches than the treasures of Egypt; for he was looking to the reward. 27 By faith he left Egypt, not fearing the wrath of the king; for he endured, **as seeing Him who is unseen**."*

Moses himself would declare that it was not merely a voice from a bush that was on fire. As he blesses the tribes in Deuteronomy 33, he asks that favor come to the head of Joseph.

*"And the choice things of the earth and its fullness, And **the favor of Him who dwelt** in the bush. Let it come to the head of Joseph..."*[100]

Clearly, Moses believes the Lord Himself was the one speaking to him from the bush.

Equally as important as understanding who was speaking to Moses from the bush is what God intended Moses to do.

A brief outline of Exodus 3

Moses confronted with God in the person of Jesus Christ-Exodus 3:1-6

We have already attempted to understand the appearance of the angel of the Lord.

God reveals His purpose to Moses- Exodus 3:7-10

The overarching purpose is to lead His people out of slavery and into the land that he had already promised (covenant with Abram).   His people would occupy that land and be His representatives (witnesses to His glory) to the world.

Moses given the authority of God's covenant name- Exodus 3:11-15

Here God reveals more than just a name to be known by. Instead, He reveals the essence of His nature. He is the uncreated One. He is from before the beginning. He is unending. The I AM WHO I AM means for whatever insufficiency Moses might have, God has abundant provision.

---

[100] Deuteronomy 33:16, NASB

Look at Jesus' own testimony in the New Testament about this Name.

John 8:24

²⁴ *Therefore I said to you that you will die in your sins; for unless you believe that I am He, you will die in your sins."*

Jesus is responding to the inquiry of the Pharisees who are asking, "Who are you?" He is at the Temple during the Feast of Tabernacles. He has just proclaimed during the lighting ceremony during the feast that he is the Light of the World.

Notice two things about this verse. First, the *He* in the verse is italicized in most translations. This indicates that it was not in the original Greek manuscripts. It has been interpreted for us. However, in trying to help us, translators may have inadvertently caused us to miss an important truth. Secondly, the Greek rendering of the phrase is consistent with the phrase from the Greek text of Exodus 3:14.

Commenting on John 8:24 John MacArthur explains...

"The Lord's use of the absolute, unqualified phrase I am (the pronoun He does not appear in the Greek text) is nothing less than a direct claim to full deity. When Moses asked God His name He replied, "I AM WHO I AM" (Ex 3:14). In the Septuagint - LXX (the Greek translation of the Old Testament), that is the same phrase (*ego eimi*) Jesus used here (the Septuagint similarly uses *ego eimi* of God in Deut 32:39; Isaiah 41:4; 43:10, 25; 45:18; 46:4). Jesus was applying to Himself the Tetragrammaton (YHWH, often transliterated as Yahweh)—the name of God that was so sacred that the Jews refused to pronounce it. Unlike many modern cult groups (such as the Jehovah's Witnesses - see notes), the Jews of Jesus' day understood perfectly that He was claiming to be God. In fact, they were so shocked by His use of that name, in reference to Himself (cf. vv. 28, 58), that they attempted to stone Him for blasphemy (v. 59)."[101]

God promises to protect and provide for His people- Exodus 3:16-22

God promises to deliver them from affliction even if it means further conflict with Pharaoh. He also promises that they will not leave their captivity empty handed but have abundant provision.

Exodus 4:24 (#18)

[24] *Now it came about at the lodging place on the way that the Lord met him and sought to put him to death.*

Here the Scripture indicates that on his way back to Egypt, after being called of God to deliver the Israelites, the Lord **met** Moses. The Hebrew word for "met" in the verse means to come into contact with, encounter, meet face to face.[102] This fact would indicate a physical meeting between Moses and the pre-incarnate Christ.

---

[101] John MacArthur, The MacArthur New Testament Commentary: John 1-11. (Chicago: Moody Press, 2006), 348.
[102] The Complete Word Study Dictionary: Old Testament, 889.

Exodus 14:19 (#19)

¹⁹ The angel of God, who had been going before the camp of Israel, moved and went behind them; and the pillar of cloud moved from before them and stood behind them.

Here Christ manifests Himself as the pillar of cloud by day and the pillar of fire by night after they fled Egypt at the Passover. Just as it was the pre-incarnate Christ in the midst of the burning bush, it was the very presence of Christ among the Israelites that accompanied them.

After they leave Egypt, the Israelites encounter many trials along the way. In **Exodus 15**, they had traveled three days in the wilderness and had found no water. When they finally did come upon water, it was too bitter to drink. The people grumbled, but Moses sought the Lord. The Lord showed him a tree that was then thrown into the water to make the water drinkable.[103]

The Lord showed the Israelites that if they followed His voice, He would take care of them. As we are, they were slow to learn. By the way, it is not a coincidence that a tree provided for the needs of the Israelites.

Exodus 17:1-7

17 Then all the congregation of the sons of Israel journeyed by stages from the wilderness of Sin, according to the command of the Lord, and camped at Rephidim, and there was no water for the people to drink. ² Therefore the people quarreled with Moses and said, "Give us water that we may drink." And Moses said to them, "Why do you quarrel

---

[103] Exodus 15:25, NASB

with me? Why do you test the Lord?" ³ *But the people thirsted there for water; and they grumbled against Moses and said, "Why, now, have you brought us up from Egypt, to kill us and our children and our livestock with thirst?"* ⁴ *So Moses cried out to the Lord, saying, "What shall I do to this people? A little more and they will stone me."* ⁵ *Then the Lord said to Moses, "Pass before the people and take with you some of the elders of Israel; and take in your hand your staff with which you struck the Nile, and go.* ⁶ *Behold, **I will stand before you** there on the rock at Horeb; and you shall strike the rock, and water will come out of it, that the people may drink." And Moses did so in the sight of the elders of Israel.* ⁷ *He named the place Massah and Meribah because of the quarrel of the sons of Israel, and because they tested the Lord, saying, "Is the Lord among us, or not?"*

The first time the Israelites had run out of water, the Bible says they grumbled at Moses. (Exodus 15:24). In this passage, they are without water again and this time they quarreled with **and** grumbled against Moses. (Exodus 17:2) The word for quarreled in the Hebrew means something much more serious than to just argue with. This word means that the Israelites brought a case against Moses, intending to take some kind of official legal action. The result of this action would lead to having Moses stoned to death. That was what Moses was afraid of in verse 4.

The issue for the Israelites, from God's perspective, was their lack of trust in His provision. Verse 5 presents a stunning picture. Realize that Moses now stands accused, even though he is the leader of the people and representative before the Lord. The Lord tells him to pass before the people, along with some of the elders and be sure to take your staff with which he had struck the Nile.

I can imagine Moses walking silently before the grumbling crowd with his staff in hand. That same staff had struck the Nile and turned its waters to blood. That same staff had been held up and the waters of the Red Sea had parted. At this point, there had to be a thought run through the minds of the grumbling Israelites that maybe they had been hasty in accusing Moses.

Edmund Clowney says of the presence of the elders, "They make up a court of judges and witnesses; their presence is necessary because of the legal formality of the situation."[104]

The full implication of what is described in verse 6 is stunning. The Lord goes on to tell Moses exactly what should happen next.

Exodus 17:6 (#20)

*6 Behold, **I will stand before you** there on the rock at Horeb; and you shall **strike the rock**, and water will come out of it, that the people may drink." And Moses did so in the sight of the elders of Israel.*

I would not be able to find any better words to describe this verse than those of Edmund Clowney. Forgive the long series of quotes, but they are worthy.

"In the Old Testament, God did not stand before men; men stood before God. In Deuteronomy the litigants in a law case were summoned to stand before the Lord and before the priests and judges (Deut. 19:17) "Before the face" of Moses the judge, with his rod uplifted, stands the God of Israel. The Lord stands in the prisoner's dock. God commands that he strike the rock. But the

---

[104] Edmund Clowney, *The Unfolding Mystery: Discovering Christ in the Old Testament* (Phillipsburg: P & R Publishing, 1988), 123.

rock is identified with God in the song of Moses: "Oh, praise the greatness of our God! He is the Rock, his works are perfect, and all his ways are just" (Deut. 32:3-4, 31)

God, the Rock, identifies Himself with the rock by standing on it. God stands in the place of the accused, and the penalty of the judgment is inflicted. Is God then guilty? No, it is the people who are guilty. In rebellion they have refused to trust the faithfulness of God. Yet God, the Judge, bears the judgment; He receives the blow that their rebellion deserves. The law must be satisfied: if God's people are to be spared, he must bear their punishment.

So, we rebels cry out in our rage. But God in His perfect righteousness has done more than the blasphemy of our cursing dares to demand. Isaiah declares, "In all their distress he too was distressed, and the angel of his presence saved them. In his love and mercy, he redeemed them; he lifted them up and carried them all the days of old. (Isaiah 63:9)

In His own Son, God came to bear our condemnation. What amazement, what awe Moses must have felt as he struck the rock of God! In God's due time that symbol was made reality. God "did not spare his own Son, but gave him up for us all" (Romans 8:32). At the cross, the Son of God took the place of His condemned people and bore the stroke of judgment. Paul rightly says of Israel in the wilderness that they "drank from the spiritual rock that accompanied them, and that rock was Christ" (1 Cor. 10:4). John tells us that Jesus stood in the Temple on the last great day of the Feast of Tabernacles and called, "if anyone is thirsty, let him come to me. And let him drink, who believes in me. As the Scripture has said, streams of living water will flow from within him" (John 7:38)

The people had cried in the accusation of unbelief, "Is the Lord among us or not?" Yes, the Lord was among them, among them in a way they could not have imagined. There He stood upon the rock; not only among them, but in their place, bearing their condemnation."[105]

The word "strike" in verse 6 is the same word that is translated "smitten" in Isaiah 53:4 which refers to Christ as our suffering servant. Also, it is the same Hebrew word that is used in Zechariah 13:7, "smite the shepherd." Jesus quotes this passage from Zechariah in Matthew 26:31 in speaking of Himself.

There is another story of the Israelites running out of water that takes place toward the end of their journey. It is a pivotal moment. It is found in the book of Numbers, chapter 20, verses 2-13.

Numbers 20:2-13

This is a different occasion than the one in Exodus. This time, the Lord tells Moses to take his staff, but to speak to the rock instead of striking it.

Moses' pride is shown in verse 10 when he says to the Israelites, "Listen now, you rebels; shall we bring forth water for you out of this rock." Clearly this shows that Moses is operating in his own power and neglecting the power and provision of the Lord.

Even though the desired result was produced, God then proclaimed to Moses that he would not bring the Israelites into the Land of Promise because Moses had not honored the Lord as Holy in the sight of the people.

---

[105] Clowney, 124-126

Of this, Clowney comments, "We do not wonder that Moses was judged severely for striking the rock a second time, when he had been told to speak to it...Only once, at His appointed time, does God bear the stroke of our doom."[106]

Moses meets often with the Lord on Mount Sinai. I have always looked at that as if Moses clawed his way up that mountain and sat there while a voice from Heaven instructed him. After studying Christ in the Old Testament, I no longer think that was the case. Consider **Deuteronomy 34:10**- "Since that time no prophet has risen in Israel like Moses, whom the Lord knew **face to face**."

Exodus 19:18-20 (#21)

[18] *Now Mount Sinai was all in smoke because **the Lord descended upon it** in fire; and its smoke ascended like the smoke of a furnace, and the whole mountain quaked violently.* [19] *When the sound of the trumpet grew louder and louder, Moses spoke and God answered him with thunder.* [20] ***The Lord came down** on Mount Sinai, to the top of the mountain; and **the Lord called Moses** to the top of the mountain, and Moses went up.*

Here again there is language of personification and what appears to be a pre-incarnate appearance of Christ. "The Lord called Moses" in verse 20 is evidence of the presence of Christ.

Exodus 24:9-11 (#22)

It is obvious from Exodus 24:9-11 that Moses, Aaron, Aaron's oldest sons and the 70 elders saw God. The question is, who did

---

they see? The Bible says that no one has seen God at any time. How can these things be reconciled?

Back in our discussion of the Trinity in Chapter 3, we learned that the persons of the Godhead, while in complete unity, are distinct persons. So, Moses and the company saw God in the person of Christ, the Son of God. They did not see the Father. Jesus Himself declared that, "If you've seen Me, you've seen the Father."[107]

This encounter made such an impression on Moses that He told the Lord that he did not want to continue toward the Promised Land, if the Lord's Presence (face) did not go with him. (Exodus 33:14-15)

The problem of Exodus 23:20-21

This can be a confusing passage. At the end of the instructions that are given to Moses by who we presume to be Christ, the Son of God, there is a pronouncement of an angel being sent to the Israelites. Who makes this pronouncement? Is Jesus promising He will send Himself as the angel? If we are to understand the Angel of the Lord as the pre-incarnate Christ, how are we to understand this passage?

Perhaps Jesus' own words would be the best interpreter. Jesus said, "I and the Father are one." (John 10:30)

God is speaking of Himself in the person of Jesus about the person of Christ. While that sounds confusing, think of it as a way to relate with mankind. God is telling the Israelites that He, Himself

---

[107] John 14:9, NASB

will go before them. But, it will have to be in a form that is condescension of the fullness of His deity.

God could not fully reveal Himself. Not that He couldn't, but the people would not be able to survive it. (Exodus 33:20) This also helps explain how the voice of the Lord was audible at the baptism of Jesus. This is a part of the mystery of the Trinity.

Verse 21 says, "since My name is in him." It was the covenant name of God that was revealed first to Moses back in Exodus 3. The name in this passage means the expression of His power and authority.

Exodus 34:5 (#23)

⁵ *The **Lord descended** in the cloud **and stood** there with him as he called upon the name of the Lord.*

This appearance occurs as a result of Moses' request to be shown the glory of the Lord in Exodus 33:18, "I pray Thee, show me Thy glory!" I believe that what Moses was asking for was a fuller revelation of the glory of God. Perhaps it was too much to ask for as Moses had already directly communed with God in the pre-incarnate Christ. Still, the same is true of us. When we have a spiritual encounter with the living God (for us through the indwelling Holy Spirit), we want something more as well.

Old Testament scholars Keil and Delitzsche write, "What Moses desired to see, as the answer of God clearly shows, must have been something surpassing all former revelations of the glory of Jehovah (Ex. 16:7, 10; 24:16-17), and even going beyond Jehovah's talking with him face to face (v. 11). When God talked with him face to face, or mouth to mouth, he merely saw a "similitude of Jehovah" (Num.

12:8), a form which rendered the invisible being of God visible to the human eye, i.e., a manifestation of the divine glory in a certain form, and not the direct or essential glory of Jehovah..."[108]

I believe the glory of God the Father is in view here. Having seen God revealed in the pre-incarnate second person of Christ, Moses realizes there is still more that has yet to be revealed. He wants to see the full revelation. However, Christ assures him that no one can see the face of God and live.[109]

James Borland writes,

"The fact that Jehovah appeared to Moses in some physical form seems to be indicated by the mention of God's "face" (v. 20), "hand" (v. 22) and "back" (v. 23). That these were not merely anthropomorphisms is shown by God's declaration that *He* would *pass by*. This passing by was to be accomplished by His "glory", which He equated with Himself in a physically perceptible manifestation (vv. 22-23). Also, Moses recorded in Exodus 34:5-9 that when the remarkable event occurred, Jehovah "*descended* in the cloud, and *stood* with him there… and the LORD *passed by* before him (italics mine). The word for "stood" … means that God placed or firmly set Himself there in a spatial relationship to Moses. Moses immediately responded by prostrating himself and worshipping before God's glorious presence (v. 8).

What seems to have happened was that God manifested Himself to Moses in a physical, apparently human-like form,

---

[108] Keil and Delitzsch, *Commentary On the Old Testament: Vol.1*, (Peabody: Hendrickson Publishers, 2011), 475.
[109] Exodus 33:20, NASB

though completely surrounded by a gloriously bright, luminous out-shining of His divine being. This brightness (as in the transfiguration of Christ, Matt. 17:2) was evidently centered in the face, which Moses was not allowed to see."[110]

I believe this passage from Exodus is in view when the Apostle John writes his gospel.

John 1:14-18

[14] *And the Word became flesh, and dwelt among us, and we saw His glory, glory as of the only begotten from the Father, full of grace and truth.* [15] *John *testified about Him and cried out, saying, "This was He of whom I said, 'He who comes after me has a higher rank than I, for He existed before me.'"* [16] *For of His fullness we have all received, and grace upon grace.* [17] *For the Law was given through Moses; grace and truth were realized through Jesus Christ.* [18] *No one has seen God at any time; the only begotten God who is in the bosom of the Father, He has explained Him.*

Verse 14 tells us that The Word (Logos), i.e. Christ, the second person of the Trinity, was made flesh (in a body like ours) and dwelt (tabernacled) among us.

It goes on to say that as a result, we beheld His glory, the glory as of the only unique Son of God.

Moses is in view here because John mentions him in verse 17. And then, I believe, refers directly to the passage in Exodus 33. In verse 18, John records, "No man has seen God at any time." Even

---

[110] James Borland, *Christ in the Old Testament: Old Testament Appearances of Christ in Human Form* (Fern, Ross-shire: Christian Focus Publications, 2010), 93.

Moses when he asked to see the fullness of God, could not endure that revelation.

John goes on to explain that the unique Son of God, who is in the bosom of the Father (eternal co-existence), has been declared (to fully reveal or declare thoroughly) by God to be God.

Paul affirms this in Colossians 1:15 and 1:19.

Colossians 1:15

And He is the image of the invisible God, the first-born of all creation.

The Greek word for image is *eikon*. This word in the Greek language always assumes a prototype. This means that Jesus as the image of God is not just one who resembles God, but, in fact, emanates from Him.

Colossians 1:19

For it was the Father's good pleasure for all the fullness to dwell in Him (Christ).

These verses affirm our fundamental assertion. It was God the Father's plan for the Son to be the full expression of Deity to humanity.

Chapter 13

Christ in the Wilderness

(Numbers-Joshua)

Numbers 11:25 (#24)

*25 Then **the Lord came down** in the cloud **and spoke** to him; and He took of the Spirit who was upon him and placed Him upon the seventy elders. And when the Spirit rested upon them, they prophesied. But they did not do it again.*

This is an interesting passage. For our purposes, we are particularly concerned with the fact that the Lord came down and spoke. That fact would constitute a pre-incarnate appearance of Christ.

However, it is interesting to note that what Christ did when He came down was to take "of the Spirit", which was upon Moses and place Him (The Holy Spirit) upon the 70 elders. So, here the pre-incarnate Christ, who is God Himself, takes some of the power of the Holy Spirit that had come to dwell upon Moses and distribute it to the elders. Notice I said, the Spirit that dwelled upon, not indwelled. I do not believe the Holy Spirit indwelled until Pentecost in Acts 2. But, it is clear from Scripture that the Holy Spirit was as present and active in the Old Testament as was Christ.

One of the most convincing texts of the pre-incarnate Christ appearing in the Old Testament is in Numbers 12:5-8. Here Aaron and Miriam were grumbling against Moses and Scripture says that the Lord came down in a pillar of cloud and **stood**.

Numbers 12:5-8 (#25)

⁵ *Then the Lord came down in a pillar of cloud and **stood** at the doorway of the tent, and He called Aaron and Miriam. When they had both come forward,* ⁶ *He said,*

"Hear now My words:

If there is a prophet among you,

I, the Lord, shall make Myself known to him in a vision.

I shall speak with him in a dream.

⁷ *"Not so, with My servant Moses,*

He is faithful in all My household;

⁸ *With him I speak mouth to mouth,*

Even openly, and not in dark sayings,

And he beholds the form of the Lord.

Why then were you not afraid

To speak against My servant, against Moses?"

Notice the words that indicate an appearance of Christ: Speaking with Moses mouth to mouth (v.8), he beholds the form of the Lord (v.8).

Numbers 22:22-35(#26)

²² *But God was angry because he was going, and **the angel of the Lord** took his stand in the way as an adversary against him. Now he was riding on his donkey and his two servants were with him.* ²³ *When the donkey saw **the angel of the Lord standing** in the way with his drawn sword in his hand, the donkey turned off from the way and went into the field; but Balaam struck the donkey to turn her back into the way.* ²⁴ *Then **the angel of the Lord stood** in a narrow path of the vineyards, with a wall on this side and a wall on that side.* ²⁵ *When the donkey saw **the angel of the Lord**, she pressed herself to the wall and pressed Balaam's foot against the wall, so he struck her again.* ²⁶ ***The angel of the Lord** went further, and stood in a narrow place where there was no way to turn to the right hand or the left.* ²⁷ *When the donkey saw **the angel of the Lord**, she lay down under Balaam; so Balaam was angry and struck the donkey with his stick.* ²⁸ *And the Lord opened the mouth of the donkey, and she said to Balaam, "What have I done to you, that you have struck me these three times?"* ²⁹ *Then Balaam said to the donkey, "Because you have made a mockery of me! If there had been a sword in my hand, I would have killed you by now."* ³⁰ *The donkey said to Balaam, "Am I not your donkey on which you have ridden all your life to this day? Have I ever been accustomed to do so to you?" And he said, "No."*

³¹ *Then the Lord opened the eyes of Balaam, and **he saw the angel of the Lord standing** in the way with his drawn sword in his hand; and he bowed all the way to the ground.* ³² ***The angel of the Lord said** to him, "Why have you struck your donkey these three times? Behold, I have come out as an adversary, because your way was contrary to me.* ³³ *But the donkey saw me and turned aside from me these three times. If she had not turned aside from me, I would surely have killed you just now, and let her live."* ³⁴ *Balaam said to **the angel of the Lord**, "I have sinned, for I did*

not know that you were standing in the way against me. Now then, if it is displeasing to you, I will turn back." **35 But the angel of the Lord said to Balaam, "Go with the men, but you shall speak only the word which I tell you."** *So Balaam went along with the leaders of Balak.*

As the Israelites journeyed toward the Promised Land, they approached the territory of the Moabites. Balak, the king of Moab was concerned about the huge number of people that were coming into his territory and feared that they may try to take over. He enlists the services of Balaam, a prophet, diviner and possessor or supernatural powers. Balak hires Balaam to put a curse on the Israelites. God, in what I believe to be the person of Christ speaks to him and warns him not to curse the Israelites.

The king of Moab is insistent and ups the ante. He offers more money and God allows Balaam to go hear the proposal, but is not pleased that he still desires to do business with the King of Moab. Along the way, several interesting things happen including the presence of the Angel of the Lord, whom we have already learned is the person of Jesus Christ in pre-incarnate form. (Numbers 22:22)

Also, Balaam's donkey could perceive the presence of the Angel of the Lord before Balaam could and refused to move forward to the point of Balaam striking the donkey three times. At this point, the Lord opened the mouth of the donkey to speak to Balaam. (Numbers 22:28)

Then, in verse 31, the Lord opens Balaam's eyes to see the Angel of the Lord. The Lord tells Balaam to go ahead and meet with Balak, but to be sure and only speak the words that the Lord tells him. (Numbers 22:35)

Balaam eventually speaks four oracles in the presence of Balak that proved to bless Israel and not curse them. In fact, each oracle contains important clues to understanding God's revelation of Himself to Balaam.

In the first oracle, Numbers 23:9, Balaam declares, "As I see him from the top of the rocks, and I look at him from the hills."

In the second oracle, Numbers 23:19, Balaam declares, "The Lord his God is with him (Israel), and the shout of a king is among them."

In the third oracle, Numbers 24:3-4, Balaam declares, "the oracle of the man whose eye is opened; The oracle of him who hears the words of God, who sees the vision of the Almighty, falling down, yet having his eyes uncovered."

The fourth oracle contains a prophecy that we must look at a bit closer.

Numbers 24:15-16 are almost identical to that of the third oracle except the phrase in verse 16 that says, "And knows the knowledge of the Most High."

Numbers 24:17

[17] *"I see him, but not now;*

I behold him, but not near;

A star shall come forth from Jacob,

A scepter shall rise from Israel,

And shall crush through the forehead of Moab,

And tear down all the sons of Sheth.

"I see him, but not now; I behold him, but not near" speaks of something that will happen in the future.

"A star shall come forth from Jacob"- Some scholars believe that Balaam's specialty was what we would know as astrology. Some even believe he was the first of what would become later known as the magi. For certain, this prophecy was connected to the magi of the New Testament's pursuit of the Messiah.

Henry Morris writes, "There is even an ancient tradition that Balaam, the notorious prophet from Mesopotamia, was an early member of the Magi, perhaps even their founder. If so, this fact would at least partially explain why the Magi at the time of Christ were aware that a special star would be used by God to announce the Savior's birth to this world."[111]

Walter Kaiser writes, "Others claim that the Magi in Matthew 2 (2:2) followed the star to Jerusalem because they believed, on the basis of Numbers 24:17, that the birth of Messiah would be marked with the appearance of a star."[112]

"And a scepter shall rise from Israel."- This would be an affirmation of Genesis 49:10 when Jacob prophesies over his sons as to the lineage of God's people and the rule of Messiah.

---

[111]
http://www.icr.org/home/resources/resources_tracts_whentheysawthestar/
[112] Walter C. Kaiser, *The Messiah in the Old Testament* (Grand Rapids: Zondervan Publishing House, 1995), 55.

Deuteronomy 31:15 (#27)

¹⁵ **The Lord appeared** *in the tent in a pillar of cloud, and the pillar of cloud stood at the doorway of the tent.*

Here the Lord appears to Moses and Joshua in the Tent of Meeting. Moses is approaching death and the Lord has chosen Joshua to lead the Israelites into the Promised Land. Joshua is commissioned to be the leader of the Israelites.

Joshua 5:13-15 (#28)

¹³ *Now it came about when Joshua was by Jericho, that he lifted up his eyes and looked, and behold, a man was standing opposite him with his sword drawn in his hand, and Joshua went to him and said to him, "Are you for us or for our adversaries?"* ¹⁴ *He said, "No; rather I indeed come now as **captain of the host of the Lord**." And Joshua fell on his face to the earth, and bowed down, and said to him, "What has my lord to say to his servant?"* ¹⁵ ***The captain of the Lord's host said*** *to Joshua, "Remove your sandals from your feet, for **the place where you are standing is holy**." And Joshua did so.*

Joshua now faces the task of leading the Israelites into occupying the Promised Land. They must totally destroy the Gentiles living in the land.

Joshua had seen this land before as he had spied it out long ago under the direction of Moses. He knew the foes would be great, he knew the cities would be powerful.

Notice in verse 10 that they observed the Passover on the fourteenth day of the month. Remember that this practice was to commemorate the deliverance of God's people from the hands of the Egyptians.

In verse 13, Joshua contemplates how to approach the conquest of the land, he looks up and sees a man with a sword drawn. Joshua, not knowing if he was a man from Jericho or one of the other Canaanite nations, asks the man about his allegiance.

Of this man, James Borland comments, "Robert B. Girdlestone notes that Joshua 'does not use the word Adam, but Ish (for the word man), which both here and elsewhere can be rendered Person or Being.' (Ish) is used in this manner in Daniel 9:21, 10:5, 12:6-7; and Zechariah 1:8, where the word is applied to beings who appear to be human, yet who are not necessarily partakers of human nature. On the contrary, the word (adam) signifies one who is a member of the race or partakes of human nature. This divine visitor partook of human characteristics and features without being at that time an actual member of the human race."[113]

The man's response was that he was the "captain of the host of the Lord." Many scholars believe that this is the pre-incarnate Christ just as He has appeared as The Angel of the Lord.

James Borland writes, "The pre-incarnate Christ met Joshua face to face as he meditated alone near Jericho."[114]

Why a different name? I believe He addresses Himself as He does and appears as He does because of what was about to take

---

[113] James Borland, *Christ in the Old Testament: Old Testament Appearances of Christ in Human Form* (Fern, Ross-shire: Christian Focus Publications, 2010), 70.
[114] Borland, 161.

place. He is bringing judgment upon the inhabitants of the land who have not obeyed or worshiped Jehovah.

Edmund Clowney writes, "Yet the Lord had not come with His sword drawn against Israel but against the wickedness of the Canaanites. The cup of their iniquity was full; the day of their judgment had arrived. The Lord did not bring Israel into the land as invading conquerors, but as avenging angels, the executors of His judgment… He came as a Warrior because His mission was to be Captain of Israel's salvation."[115]

Joshua's response to the man gives the clearest evidence that this was no mere man or angel.

In verse 14, Joshua fell on his face and bowed down. This was the same response that Abram had when he encountered Christ in Genesis 18.

At the same time, Joshua said to the man, "What has my lord to say to his servant?" At this time, the only lord and master that Joshua had was **The** Lord.

Of equal importance is the Lord's reply back to Joshua, "Remove your sandals from your feet, for the place where you are standing is holy. And Joshua did so."[116]

Again, James Borland writes, "The words are practically a duplication of God's command to Moses at the burning bush. No

---

[115] Edmund Clowney, *The Unfolding Mystery: Discovering Christ in the Old Testament* (Phillipsburg: P & R Publishing, 1988), 131.
[116] Joshua 5:15, NASB.

created angel makes such demands, but God's presence sanctifies the area."[117]

---

[117] Borland, 161.

Chapter 14

Christt Among the Judges

(Judges)

In stark contrast to faithful Joshua, the Israelites were mired in rebellion after his death. The book of Judges spans 400 years of history and seven cycles of rebellion to deliverance.

Judges 2:1 (#29)

*Now **the angel of the Lord** came up from Gilgal to Bochim. **And he said**, "I brought you up out of Egypt and led you into the land which I have sworn to your fathers; and I said, 'I will never break My covenant with you."*

Here again we see the Angel of the Lord. Notice the language used to describe the movement, "Now the Angel of the Lord came up from Gilgal to Bochim."

The Hebrew word for "came up" means to ascend implying either upward motion or a northerly direction. I would contend that this again shows the personification of the Angel of the Lord. It is as if He is walking north or ascending a height from Gilgal to Bochim.

Gilgal is that place where the Israelites camped after crossing the Jordan. It was a monumental place for them. There is significance in the fact that the Angel of the Lord was in Gilgal and had to come up to where the Israelites were in Bochim.

By the way, the people had not yet named this place Bochim. They do that in verse five of this chapter in response to the words that were spoken to them by the Angel of the Lord.

Scholars do not agree as to the exact location of Bochim, especially since this is the only place in Scripture where the name is mentioned. Most scholars fall into one of two camps as to Bochim's location, near Bethel or near Shiloh. Whichever of those two places, there would certainly be either an ascent up a mountain or in a northerly direction.

The most significant aspect of this passage, however, is not where the Angel came from, but what He said. Again, let me remind you that this is the pre-incarnate Christ speaking these words to the people of Israel. "I will never break My covenant with you."

It is much more powerful a thought that the pre-incarnate Christ, the second person of the Godhead, would be the one reminding the Israelites that He will not break His covenant. It is not just an angelic messenger speaking. It is God Himself.

Christ speaks to them and tells them that He will not drive out the inhabitants of the land because of Israel's unfaithfulness. Thus, the people of Israel will struggle against man and God from then on.

Judges 6:11-12, 20-22 (#30)

¹¹ Then the angel of the Lord came and sat under the oak that was in Ophrah, which belonged to Joash the Abiezrite as his son Gideon was beating out wheat in the wine press in order to save it from the Midianites. ¹² The angel of the Lord appeared to him and said to him, "The Lord is with you, O valiant warrior." ²⁰ The angel of God said to him, "Take the meat and the unleavened bread and lay them on this rock, and pour out the broth." And he did so. ²¹ Then the angel of the Lord put out the end of the staff that was in his hand and touched the meat and the unleavened bread; and fire sprang up from the rock and consumed the meat and the unleavened bread. Then the angel of the Lord vanished from his sight. ²² When Gideon saw that he was the angel of the Lord, he said, "Alas, O Lord God! For now I have seen the angel of the Lord face to face."

Following the rule of Deborah and Barak, the Bible says the land was undisturbed for forty years before they again did evil in the sight of the Lord.

As a result, He gave them into the hands of the Midianites for seven years.

In verse 8 of chapter 6, there is another piece of evidence that shows the difference between a messenger form God and the Angel of the Lord. When the Angel of the Lord spoke to the Israelites in chapter 1, He simply spoke to them authoritatively. In verse 8 of chapter 6, Scripture says the Lord sent a prophet who then said, "Thus says the Lord, the God of Israel."

But, according to His promise to them to never break His covenant, the Angel of the Lord appears to a man named Gideon in verse 11 and following.

In verse 11, notice the personification in that the Angel of the Lord **sat.**

In verse 12, notice the irony. The Lord called him Valiant Warrior. Verse 15 tells us that according to his own admission, Gideon's family was the least in Manasseh and he was the youngest in the family.

The Angel of the lord also proclaims to him that Jehovah is with him. I'm sure at this point Gideon did not understand the true nature of what he had been told.

In verse 13, Gideon replied respectfully, "O my lord" (adon) This was the common word for master or anyone in authority. He uses a different word in his question at the end of the verse, "Didn't "Jehovah" bring us up…"

In verse 14, the Lord looked at him. Literally "turned toward him" and said, "Have I not sent you?"

In verse 15, Gideon uses a different word in reply, "O Lord"- (adonay) My Lord. This is the same word Abraham used when the pre-incarnate Christ appeared to him at another oak tree in Mamre. (Genesis 18:3) This word, according to the Word Study Dictionary, is used exclusively of God.[118]

At this point it starts to dawn on Gideon who he might be speaking with, but he is not quite convinced. So, he asks for a sign.

In verse 18, Scripture says, "Do not depart from here, until I come back to Thee and bring out my offering and lay it before Thee." The Lord replies, "I will remain until you return"

---

[118] The Word Study Dictionary: Old Testament, 18.

In verse 21 Gideon returns with his offering and the Lord instructs him how he was to lay it out before Him. The Lord touches the offering with His staff and fire sprang up and consumed the offering.

The end of verse 21 reads, "Then the Angel of the Lord vanished from his sight." This is an unfortunate translation. It makes it appear that the Lord just performed a magic trick and then with a turn of His cloak made Himself disappear. This is not the way the Hebrew reads.

The words in the Hebrew mean that the Lord moved out of Gideon's sight. He did not vanish, but just moved out of his line of sight. Isn't that what the Lord promised He would do in verse 18?

Verse 22 says, "When Gideon saw that he was the Angel of the Lord." Notice how his words change again, "Alas, O Lord God." This is a form of the covenant name of God used by The Lord Himself when He met Moses at the burning bush. The Word Study Dictionary says it means, "He who is or is present." [119] This was quite a change from the simple name lord, i.e. master as he first addressed the Lord.

Of course, Gideon led the people of Israel to defeat the Midianites in God's power.

Notice that in this passage, there are what could be the activity of all three persons of the Trinity. Verse 34 says, "The Spirit of the Lord came upon Gideon" and God performed a miracle with the test of Gideon's fleece in verse 40.

---

[119] The Word Study Dictionary: Old Testament, 426-427.

Judges 13:1-22 (#31)

Now the sons of Israel again did evil in the sight of the Lord, so that the Lord gave them into the hands of the Philistines forty years.

*² There was a certain man of Zorah, of the family of the Danites, whose name was Manoah; and his wife was barren and had borne no children. ³ Then **the angel of the Lord appeared** to the woman and said to her, "Behold now, you are barren and have borne no children, but you shall conceive and give birth to a son. ⁴ Now therefore, be careful not to drink wine or strong drink, nor eat any unclean thing.⁵ For behold, you shall conceive and give birth to a son, and no razor shall come upon his head, for the boy shall be a Nazirite to God from the womb; and he shall begin to deliver Israel from the hands of the Philistines." ⁶ Then the woman came and told her husband, saying, "A man of God came to me and **his appearance was like the appearance of the angel of God**, very awesome. And I did not ask him where he came from, nor did he tell me his name. ⁷ But he said to me, 'Behold, you shall conceive and give birth to a son, and now you shall not drink wine or strong drink nor eat any unclean thing, for the boy shall be a Nazirite to God from the womb to the day of his death.'"*

*⁸ Then Manoah entreated the Lord and said, "O Lord, please let the man of God whom You have sent come to us again that he may teach us what to do for the boy who is to be born." ⁹ God listened to the voice of Manoah; and **the angel of God came again to the woman** as she was sitting in the field, but Manoah her husband was not with her. ¹⁰ So the woman ran quickly and told her husband, "Behold, the man who came the other day has appeared to me." ¹¹ Then Manoah arose and followed his wife, and when he came to the man he said to him, "Are you the man who spoke to the woman?" And he said, "I am." ¹² Manoah said, "Now when* your words come to pass, what shall be the boy's mode of life and his vocation?" ¹³ So **the angel of the Lord said** to Manoah, "Let the woman pay attention to all that I said. ¹⁴ She should not eat anything that comes from the vine nor drink wine or strong drink, nor eat any unclean thing; let her observe all that I commanded."

¹⁵ Then **Manoah said to the angel of the Lord**, "Please let us detain you so that we may prepare a young goat for you." ¹⁶ **The angel of the Lord said** to Manoah, "Though you detain me, I will not eat your food, but if you prepare a burnt offering, then offer it to the Lord." For Manoah did not know that **he was the angel of the Lord**. ¹⁷ Manoah said to **the angel of the Lord**, "What is your name, so that when your words come to pass, we may honor you?" ¹⁸ But **the angel of the Lord said to him**, "Why do you ask my name, seeing it is wonderful?" ¹⁹ So Manoah took the young goat with the grain offering and offered it on the rock to the Lord, and He performed wonders while Manoah and his wife looked on. ²⁰ For it came about when the flame went up from the altar toward heaven, that **the angel of the Lord ascended** in the flame of the altar. When Manoah and his wife saw this, they fell on their faces to the ground.

²¹ Now **the angel of the Lord** did not appear to Manoah or his wife again. Then Manoah knew that he was the angel of the Lord. ²² So Manoah said to his wife, "We will surely die, for **we have seen God**."

Again, the Israelites found themselves in captivity, this time to the Philistines.

In verses 2-4, the Angel of the Lord appeared to Manoah's wife and told her she would bear a son. It's interesting that we are never told the name of Manoah's wife.

In verse 5, we are told that the child was to be raised as a Nazirite (Numbers 6:1-8). A Nazirite was one who vowed to be separated to God. In addition, verse 5 reveals the purpose of God for Samson.

In verse 6, Manoah's wife indicated that the appearance of the "man of God" was very awesome. The KJV uses the word terrible. The Hebrew word means to be feared or reverenced, held in high esteem.

Once the Angel of the Lord appeared again so that Manoah could encounter him, Manoah wanted to prepare Him a meal. Verse 16 tells us that Manoah still did not know it was the Angel of the Lord.

In verses 17-18, Manoah asked the name of the Angel of the Lord. He responded, "Why do you ask my name seeing it is wonderful?" The word Wonderful or, incomprehensible, is also used in Psalm 139:6 "Such knowledge is too wonderful for me." The word is also translated "secret." The more familiar use of this word is found in Isaiah 9, "His name shall be called "Wonderful Counselor, Mighty God..."[120]

Verse 19 tells us that the Lord "performed wonders" there with the lamb of the offering. We have no certainty as to what this may have been. It cannot, however, be a coincidence that the pre-incarnate Christ was presented a lamb offered to the lord on a rock. What would He have done with that lamb?

The Word Study Dictionary says of the Hebrew word "wonders" used here and as "wondrously" in the KJV, "While

---

[120] Isaiah 9:6, NASB.

nothing is too extraordinary for God, various things are said to be beyond the abilities of some individuals to do or comprehend...A rare use of this Hebrew word expresses the performance of a special vow beyond the ordinary commitment."[121]

Verse 20 tells us that the Angel of the Lord ascended in a flame toward Heaven and when Manoah and his wife saw this they fell on their faces to the ground, presumably in worship.

At that point, verse 21 records that Manoah knew it was the Angel of the Lord.

Verse 22 says, Manoah said to his wife, "We shall surely die for we have seen God."

Of course, we know that the child that the Lord promised to Manoah and his wife would be the mighty Samson who, flawed though he may have been, God displayed in him mighty acts of valor.

Why would God choose to use someone mightily who made so many terrible choices?

One could ask that question about any of us. But, just look at the people that God chose to use throughout the Scripture. Noah was a drunk, Abraham was a liar and an adulterer, Moses was a murderer, David committed manslaughter and adultery, Peter denied Christ, Paul killed Christians. The list could go on, but yet God used every single one and many more, even you and me.

---

[121] The Word Study Dictionary: Old Testament, 899.

Through all of the chaos, God accomplished His purpose that He set out to accomplish in 13:5, to deliver Israel from the hands of the Philistines.

Two statements from A.B. Simpson provide a fitting conclusion to this story:[122]

Samson was, "a marvelous example of what God might have done with a thoroughly separated, and yet of what self-indulgence and sin can do to hinder the glorious promise and the gracious purpose of God."

"It is a very solemn and awful thing to think how we can hinder God's purposes of love for us. This is an important lesson. Despite the fact that we may have been born to Christian parents who brought us up to fear God; despite the fact that our early days were overshadowed by the Almighty and our consciousnesses felt the touch of heaven and heard the whisper of His calling on our lives; we may, by our willfulness and folly, destroy all this."

Is it any wonder that we still fall and stray? After all, even those who have seen God face to face in the person of Christ, still manage to find a way to stumble.

---

[122] A.B. Simpson, *The Christ in the Bible Commentary, Vol.2* (Camp Hill: Christian Publications, 1992), 205.

Chapter 15

Christ Among the Kings

(1 & 2 Samuel, 1 & 2 Kings, 1 & 2 Chronicles)

T he time of the Kings of Israel and Judah were particularly turbulent for the people of God. Each succession of a new King brought more uncertainty as to the degree in which they would hold fast to the commands of the Lord. If the Kings were to lead God's people, yet the kings did not follow His law, how were the people to learn how to walk with God?

First, we should not that, according to 1 Samuel 3:1 that "word from the Lord was rare in those days." Something in the life of the Hebrew people was changing since the time of the judges and before kings began to reign. Truly it was a dark and difficult time.

We are introduced to a man named Elkanah, of the tribe of Ephraim, who would worship yearly at Shiloh with his two wives, Hannah and Peninnah. Yes, that's right, two wives. I would imagine that the reason there are two wives is the necessity of extending the family lineage since Hannah was barren. (1 Samuel 1:2) Because of the order of the names, we can safely assume that Elkanah had married Hannah first and since she was barren had then married Peninnah in order to carry on the family line.

Notice that they would go to Shiloh to worship. Joshua 18:1 reveals that the tent of meeting, the place of Hebrew worship, was located in Shiloh. Remember a very important point of prophecy in Genesis 49:10. "The scepter shall not depart from Judah, nor the ruler's staff from between his feet until Shiloh comes."

The name Shiloh means, "the one to whom it belongs." Shiloh is a reference to Christ. So, here the scepter continues.

Elkanah is said to sacrifice to "the Lord of hosts." This is a specific name of God that appears here for the first time. It is not found in Scripture until this verse. The NIV translates it as "The Lord Almighty." The name means, in the Hebrew, "Yahweh, the God of the armies of Heaven." From this point forward, this name of God will be used 261 times in the Old Testament. It shows that He is the supreme ruler. I believe it is no coincidence that this name for God appears here just before Israel begs for a king to be like other nations.

Apparently, Peninnah made life very difficult for the barren Hannah and Hannah grieved over not being able to have a child. She prayed to the Lord at the temple and was found by Eli, the priest. She was apparently so distraught that he assumed her to be drunk. Eli joined her in praying for God to allow her to bear, specifically, a son. In verse 11, she vows to dedicate this son to the Lord if the Lord will allow her to give birth.

In verse 20, we read that the Lord answered her prayer and gave her a son whom she named, Samuel. The name Samuel was quite a mystery for a long time as to its meaning. We have the evidence of Scripture in verse 20 that gives the meaning according to Hannah's thoughts, "Because I asked him of the Lord."

Many modern translators have said that the name Samuel simply means, "name of God." However, A.M. Hodgkin writes, "The meaning of his name was one of the perplexities of Hebrew scholarship till the year 1899, when the Twelfth Congress of Orientalists held its meeting at Rome, and Professor Jastrow of Philadelphia, showed that, in the Assyrian, which is closely allied to the Hebrew tongue, the word *sumu* means *son*, and he translated Samuel as 'son (or offspring) of God.' Hannah, in the depth and sincerity of her surrender, gave up her first-born son to God utterly."[123]

1 Samuel 2

In chapter 2, Hannah prays a beautiful prayer of Thanksgiving for God answering her prayer and giving her a son. In fact, when compared to Mary's song, in Luke 1:46-55, you will see much of the same thoughts. It is quite a comparison of the two events. The prayer contains quite a bit of theology, much more than some scholars think possible for the humble Hannah.

It is an important lesson for us, however, because most of the things that Hannah praises God for and says of Him, are things which she had heard of Him to do. The lesson for us is that for our prayer life to be as powerful as Hannah, we must have a proper knowledge of God from reading, understanding and memorizing the Word of God. To ask Him to do something in the present or future for us, we must be very familiar with what he has done in the past.

---

[123] A.M. Hodgkins, *Christ in All the Scriptures* (Forgotten Books, 2012), 63.

In verse 10, we find a reference to the Messiah. "The Lord will judge the ends of the earth; And He will give strength to His king, And He will exalt the horn of His anointed." The word anointed in this verse means, "Messiah."

1 Samuel 3:10, 21 (#32)

*¹⁰ Then the Lord **came and stood and called** as at other times, "Samuel! Samuel!" And Samuel said, "Speak, for Your servant is listening... ²¹ And **the Lord appeared again at Shiloh**, because the Lord revealed Himself to Samuel at Shiloh by the word of the Lord.*

In chapter 3, we find Samuel ministering in the tent of meeting/temple with Eli. And, one night, Samuel hears his name being called three times.

In verse 10, the third time he hears his name, the Bible says, "Then the Lord came and stood and called as at other times..."

Here we have personification of God, a Christophany, especially with the word "stood."

James Borland writes, "The combination of these three words ('came', 'stood', 'called') confirms the idea that God was physically manifested to little Samuel."[124]

He goes on to quote Arthur Hervey, "A personal Presence, not a mere voice, or impression upon Samuel's mind, is thus distinctly indicated." And then Borland writes, "Keil and Delitzsch agree,

---

[124] James Borland, *Christ in the Old Testament: Old Testament Appearances of Christ in Human Form* (Fern, Ross-shire: Christian Focus Publications, 2010), 84.

saying, 'These words show that the revelation of God was an objectively real affair, and not a mere dream of Samuel's."[125]

Furthermore, in verse 21, the Bible says, "And the Lord appeared again at Shiloh, because the Lord revealed Himself to Samuel at Shiloh by the word of the Lord." The word "word," in the verse, means speech.

Samuel would go on to be the instrument of the Lord in bringing David to the throne.

2 Samuel 24:16 (#33)

[16] *When **the angel stretched out his hand** toward Jerusalem to destroy it, the Lord relented from the calamity and said to the angel who destroyed the people, "It is enough! Now relax your hand!" And **the angel of the Lord was by the threshing floor** of Araunah the Jebusite."*

This is a difficult passage, and some would not include this as a viable Christophany.[126] This text has a parallel passage in 1 Chronicles 21 in which additional information is given. The background of the passage is that, according to 1 Chronicles 21:1, "Satan stood up against Israel and moved David to number Israel." Most scholars would agree that this is not a possession of David, but merely David giving in to the temptation presented by Satan.

It is not unclear why numbering Israel was such a detestable thing in the eyes of the Lord. Keil and Delitzsch offer a satisfying

---

[125] Borland, 84-85.
[126] James Borland for instance in *Christ in The Old Testament: Old Testament Appearances of Christ in Human Form* includes this passage in a list of which he says there are no peculiar marks of deity noted.

explanation. "The true kernel of David's sin was to be found, no doubt, in self-exaltation, inasmuch as he sought for the strength and glory of his kingdom in the number of the people and their readiness for war."[127]

Whatever the reason for God's displeasure, the end result was that He would punish Israel.[128] Apparently, here, the pre-incarnate Christ as the Angel of the Lord is His instrument in executing that punishment. In the parallel account, the Angel of the Lord is seen as wielding a sword (1 Chronicles 21:16). The Apostle John's vision of Christ also contains a two-edged sword proceeding form the mouth of the Messiah/King.[129]

Michael P.V. Barrett writes, "According to 2 Samuel 24:16 (see also 1 Chronicles 21:16), it was the Angel of the Lord that executed the plague judgment on Israel after David's sin of numbering the people. Interestingly, in this passage it is clear that the Lord assigned the role of executing judge to the Angel...Remember that the Lord Jesus said that the Father had given him "authority to execute judgment also, because he is the Son of man" (John 5:27)."[130]

It is also worthwhile to notice one other significant aspect of this passage. First, verse 16 mentions that the Angel of the Lord was "by the threshing floor of Araunah the Jebusite." The Jebusites were the ones who formerly occupied the land of Jerusalem, prior

---

[127] Keil and Delitzsch, *Commentary on the Old Testament, vol. 2* (Peabody, Mass:Hendrickson Publishers, 2011), 706.
[128] 1 Chronicles 21:7, NASB
[129] Revelation 1:16, NASB
[130] Michael P.V. Barrett, *Beginning at Moses: A Guide to Finding Christ in the Old Testament* (Greenville:Ambassador-Emerald International, 2001), 158.

to the Israelites entrance into the Promised Land. God had promised that land to the descendants of Abraham (Genesis 12) and commanded that all of the occupants of Canaan be exterminated (Leviticus 18:24-25). So, here is a Canaanite, who should have been "removed" from this land that was promised to the people of God and he owns a piece of property that David now wants to purchase. Araunah wants to just give the King the land (perhaps in fear for his life). That piece of property was on Mount Moriah, where Abraham was to sacrifice Isaac until the Angel of the Lord stopped his hand from plunging the knife into the son of promise. Here, the Angel of the Lord, the pre-incarnate Son of God, is back at the same place as He executes judgment against Israel with a sword. Furthermore, this same piece of land would be the location where Solomon would build the Temple.

1 Kings 19:5-7 (#34)

*⁵ He lay down and slept under a juniper tree; and behold, there was **an angel** touching him, and he said to him, "Arise, eat." ⁶ Then he looked and behold, there was at his head a bread cake baked on hot stones, and a jar of water. So he ate and drank and lay down again. ⁷ **The angel of the Lord came again a second time** and touched him and said, "Arise, eat, because the journey is too great for you."*

The prophet Elijah finds himself hiding despondently under a Juniper Tree filled with fear that King Ahab will find him. In reality, he may have feared Jezebel more than Ahab. Ahab's wife, Jezebel, was the one making threats to end Elijah's life. Elijah had just demonstrated his faith in Almighty God in a showdown with the prophets of the false god, Baal. Ahab, King of Israel, had ceased following Jehovah God and began to worship Baal.

141

²⁹ *Now Ahab the son of Omri became king over Israel in the thirty-eighth year of Asa king of Judah, and Ahab the son of Omri reigned over Israel in Samaria twenty-two years.* ³⁰ *Ahab the son of Omri did evil in the sight of the Lord more than all who were before him.*

³¹ *It came about, as though it had been a trivial thing for him to walk in the sins of Jeroboam the son of Nebat, that he married Jezebel the daughter of Ethbaal king of the Sidonians, and went to serve Baal and worshiped him.* ³² *So he erected an altar for Baal in the house of Baal which he built in Samaria.* ³³ *Ahab also made the Asherah. Thus Ahab did more to provoke the Lord God of Israel than all the kings of Israel who were before him.*[131]

Now, finding Elijah in fear for his life, Christ, as the Angel of the Lord finds him under the Juniper Tree. The Angel of the Lord ministered to Elijah two different times and encouraged him to continue on to Horeb, the mountain of God. The Lord still had plans to use Elijah.

2 Kings 1:3, 15 (#35)

³ *But **the angel of the Lord said** to Elijah the Tishbite, "Arise, go up to meet the messengers of the king of Samaria and say to them, 'Is it because there is no God in Israel that you are going to inquire of Baal-zebub, the god of Ekron?'*

¹⁵ ***The angel of the Lord said** to Elijah, "Go down with him; do not be afraid of him." So he arose and went down with him to the king.*

After Ahab's death, his son Ahaziah became King of Israel. He followed in his father's footsteps, not only by becoming King, but

---

[131] 1 Kings 16:29-33, NASB.

by serving and worshiping Baal instead of Jehovah God. After falling through the lattice in his chamber, Ahaziah became ill. Instead of inquiring of The Lord, he sent messengers to go and inquire of Baal-zebub, the god of Ekron.[132]

Christ, The Angel of the Lord, gave Elijah the message that, because Azariah inquired of a false god, instead of Jehovah, he would not recover from his illness and would die. The Bible says, "So Ahaziah died according to the word of the Lord which Elijah had spoken."[133]

2 Kings 19:35 (#36)

*[35] Then it happened that night that **the angel of the Lord** went out and struck 185,000 in the camp of the Assyrians; and when men rose early in the morning, behold, all of them were dead.*

Here we find Sennacherib, King of Assyria, having already taken the Northern Kingdom of Israel into captivity, threatening the same for the Kingdom of Judah. Rather than giving in and trusting his own intellect and power, King Hezekiah seeks out wisdom from the prophet Isaiah and from the Lord Himself.

[15] Hezekiah prayed before the Lord and said, "O Lord, the God of Israel, who are enthroned above the cherubim, You are the God, You alone, of all the kingdoms of the earth. You have made heaven and earth. [16] Incline Your ear, O Lord, and hear; open Your eyes, O Lord, and see; and listen to the words of Sennacherib, which he has sent to reproach the living God. (2 Kings 19:15-16)

---

[132] 2 Kings 2:2
[133] 2 Kings 1:17, NASB.

The Lord spoke through Isaiah (about Sennacherib), *"Behold, I will put a spirit in him so that he will hear a rumor and return to his own land. And I will make him fall by the sword in his own land."*[134] During that very night that Hezekiah prayed, the Angel of the Lord struck down 185,000 Assyrians. As a result, Sennacherib turned back toward Nineveh where he would be murdered by one of his sons.[135]

2 Chronicles 7:12 (#37)

[12] *Then* **the Lord appeared** *to Solomon at night and said to him, "I have heard your prayer and have chosen this place for Myself as a house of sacrifice.*

According to 1 Kings 11:9, the Lord appeared to King Solomon on two occasions.

[9] *Now the Lord was angry with Solomon because his heart was turned away from* **the Lord, the God of Israel, who had appeared to him twice,**

There are three verses of Scripture that represent these two appearances. In the first appearance, The Lord appears to Solomon in a dream at night.

[5] *In Gibeon* **the Lord appeared to Solomon in a dream** *at night; and God said, "Ask what you wish Me to give you."* (I Kings 3:15)

At this appearance, Solomon asked the Lord for discernment on how to judge the people of God.

---

[134] 2 Kings 19:7, NASB.
[135] 2 Kings 19:37, NASB.

⁹ So give Your servant an understanding heart to judge Your people to discern between good and evil. For who is able to judge this great people of Yours?"[136]

Apparently, this was not a physical appearance of the pre-incarnate Christ because it was in a dream. Thus, it does not fit into the scope of the numbering of pre-incarnate appearances according to this work.

The second appearance, however, is recorded in two passages, 1 Kings 9:2 and 2 Chronicles 7:12.

² that the Lord appeared to Solomon a second time, as He had appeared to him at Gibeon. – 1 Kings 9:2

¹² Then **the Lord appeared** *to Solomon at night and said to him, "I have heard your prayer and have chosen this place for Myself as a house of sacrifice. –* 2 Chronicles 7:12

Neither one of these verses uses the word "dream" to describe the appearance of the Lord. However, the 1 Kings passage does indicate that the Lord appeared to Solomon, *"as He had appeared to him at Gibeon."* This has led some scholars to determine that it was a second appearance of the same kind as the first. For example, Keil and Delitzsch write, "When Solomon had finished the building of the temple, and of his palace, and of all that he had a desire to build, the Lord appeared to him a second time, as He had appeared to him at Gibeon, *i.e., by night in a dream (italics mine)."*[137]

---

[136] 1 Kings 3:9, NASB.
[137] Keil and Delitzsch, *Commentary on the Old Testament, vol. 3* (Peabody, Mass:Hendrickson Publishers, 2011), 98.

Had this been the only other verse describing this event, I would wholeheartedly agree with Keil and Delitzsch. However, because of a second description of this same event and the absence, still, of a direct indication of a dream, I conclude that this was a pre-incarnate appearance of Christ.

Chapter 16

Christt Among the Prophets

(Jeremiah and Daniel)

Perhaps because the Kings found it difficult to both rule and be submissive to God, God sent prophets to speak to the Kings messages that the Lord wanted them to hear. Thus, the prophets became the primary method for the voice of God to the king and God's people.

Over and over in The Old Testament, the prophets declared, "The Lord said to me," "Thus says the Lord" and "The Word of the Lord came to me." We cannot say with certainty if these were direct pre-incarnate appearances. For example, are we to interpret, "The Word of the Lord came to me" as to mean that Christ, the Logos or Word, came and spoke with me and told me to say this and that? Or, does it simply mean that they were guided and directed by the Holy Spirit to write the words down?

One interpretive hint from the New Testament comes from the Apostle Peter, *"But know this first of all, that no prophecy of Scripture is a matter of one's own interpretation, for no prophecy was ever made by an act of human will, but men moved by the Holy Spirit spoke from God."*[138]

---

[138] 2 Peter 1:20-21, NASB.

John M. Burris

The prophet Jeremiah records this interaction with the Lord, *"Then the Lord stretched out His hand and **touched** my mouth, and the Lord said to me, Behold, I have put My words in your mouth."*[139] Does this mean that Jeremiah had a direct physical contact with the pre-incarnate Christ?

Numbers 12:6-8 gives us what may be the most definitive explanation of how God spoke to the prophets.

"⁶ He said,

"Hear now My words:

If there is a prophet among you,

I, the Lord, shall make Myself known to him in a vision.

I shall speak with him in a dream.

⁷ "Not so, with My servant Moses,

He is faithful in all My household;

⁸ With him I speak mouth to mouth,

Even openly, and not in dark sayings,

And he beholds the form of the Lord."

So, it seems that the normal method for God communicating to His people through the prophets would have been through dreams and visions. And, Moses, as we have already seen, would have been an exception to that norm because the Lord spoke with him face to face.

---

[139] Jeremiah 1:9, NASB.

148

With this in mind, there are only a few pre-incarnate appearances of Christ in the books of the major and minor prophets. Of course, Elijah was a prophet and we have already identified his encounters with the pre-incarnate Christ in chapter 15.

Jeremiah 1:4-10 (#38)

⁴ *Now the word of the Lord came to me saying,*

⁵ *"Before I formed you in the womb I knew you,*

And before you were born I consecrated you;

I have appointed you a prophet to the nations."

⁶ *Then I said, "Alas, Lord God!*

Behold, I do not know how to speak,

Because I am a youth."

⁷ *But the Lord said to me,*

"Do not say, 'I am a youth,'

Because everywhere I send you, you shall go,

And all that I command you, you shall speak.

⁸ *"Do not be afraid of them,*

For I am with you to deliver you," declares the Lord.

⁹ ***Then the Lord stretched out His hand and touched my mouth,*** *and the Lord said to me,*

"Behold, I have put My words in your mouth.

[10] *"See, I have appointed you this day over the nations and over the kingdoms,*

To pluck up and to break down,

To destroy and to overthrow,

To build and to plant."

I almost did not include this account in the list of Christophanies. Frankly, I would not have included it if it were not for verse 9, ***"Then the Lord stretched out His hand and touched my mouth."*** It is fascinating to consider exactly how the prophets of God received the instructions from God. Was it in prayer? Was it a vision? Did they just hear a voice? Or was it the visible presence of God in the person of Christ?

Michael S. Heiser affirms this account as a prophecy, "Jeremiah identifies this Word as Yahweh himself when he replies, 'Ah, Lord Yahweh!... then something shocking happens. Jeremiah writes in v. 9 that Yahweh, the Word, 'stretched out his hand and he touched my mouth. Sounds don't reach out and touch people. This is the language of a physical, embodied presence."[140]

Daniel 3:23-25 (#39)

[23] *But these three men, Shadrach, Meshach and Abed-nego, fell into the midst of the furnace of blazing fire still tied up.*

[24] *Then Nebuchadnezzar the king was astounded and stood up in haste; he said to his high officials, "Was it not three men we cast bound into the midst of the fire?" They replied to the king, "Certainly, O king."* [25] *He*

---

[140] Michael S. Heiser, *The Unseen Realm:Recovering the Supernatural Worldview of the Bible* (Bellingham, WA: Lexham Press, 2015), 132.

said, "Look! I see four men loosed and walking about in the midst of the fire without harm, and **the appearance of the fourth is like a son of the gods!"**

The Southern Kingdom of Judah has been taken into captivity in Babylon. Now the people of God are once again under the rule of a pagan nation. King Nebuchadnezzar, the King of Babylon constructed a massive statue of himself on the plain of Dura. He commanded the whole kingdom to come and bow down before the statue and worship the image, including God's people who are to worship and serve Him only.

The image is sixty cubits tall. A cubit is about 18 inches. So, the statue is about 90 feet tall. To give you perspective, Cristo Redentor, or Christ the Redeemer statue in Rio De Janeiro, Brazil is 98 feet tall.

Three Hebrew men, you know them as Shadrach, Meshach and Abed-nego, but their Hebrew names were Hananiah, Mishael and Azariah, are reported to the king to not have bowed down and worshipped the image of Nebuchadnezzar.

v. 15- Nebuchadnezzar warns them that if they don't bow and worship, they will be cast into a furnace of blazing fire. Why would there be a furnace of blazing fire there near the statue on the plain of Dura? Perhaps, it was used in the construction of the statue or perhaps it had something to do with the rituals of the pagan worship of the Babylonians.

v.16- The Hebrew men didn't even need to think about it. Their minds were already made up. We have to have that same conviction about how we are to respond to temptation. We must be already resolved to obey.

v.17- *"Our God, whom we serve is able to deliver us from the furnace of blazing fire."* Notice that they don't even fear that they will die and be received by God, they fully expect Him to deliver them.

So, they were cast into the fire, which was so hot that the men who were charged with throwing them into the fire, were killed. The furnace would have been either an ore smelter or a kiln used for curing brick. Nebuchadnezzar ordered it to be heated seven times hotter than usual. The fact that it was previously heated (since now it was seven times hotter), suggests that this was a furnace used in the making of the statue.

vv.24-25- As Nebuchadnezzar watches their demise, he realizes that something was not as it should have been...there were **four** men, loosed, walking about in the fire and the appearance of the fourth is like a son of the gods.

I believe this was the pre-incarnate Christ walking around the furnace with Hananiah, Mishael and Azariah. Remember that they had said "our God" is able to deliver us. We have no reason to doubt that they were witnesses to the personal deliverance of the God of Israel in the person of Jesus Christ.

Look at what the prophet Isaiah, 150 years before the events of Daniel 3, prophesied.

Isaiah 43:1-2

"But now, thus says the Lord, your Creator, O Jacob,

And He who formed you, O Israel,

"Do not fear, for I have redeemed you;

I have called you by name; you are Mine!

"When you pass through the waters, I will be with you;

And through the rivers, they will not overflow you.

When you walk through the fire, you will not be scorched,

Nor will the flame burn you."

Perhaps the reason why there are only a few passages that refer to an "appearance" of the pre-incarnate Christ in the Prophets is the circumstances surrounding the place and people described, a pagan nation with no prophet. Daniel is not mentioned in the passage so there is no prophet of God present. God, being certain to keep the promise made in Isaiah 43 (of walking through the fire and not being scorched), sends the pre-incarnate Christ into the fire with Hananiah, Mishael and Azariah. It was essential for God to keep His Word.

Most of the descriptions or allusions to Christ in the Prophets are contained in dreams and visions. Passages such as, Isaiah 6, Daniel 10:10 and Zecharaiah 1:8-12, 3:1-6 and 12:8 all clearly describe Christ. But, since they were contained in visions or dreams, I do not consider them to be pre-incarnate appearances.

Conclusion

So what? That could be one of the most common questions after one of my Bible Studies (I tend to lean toward examination rather than application). But, really, what difference does it make just when Christ "appeared" in the Old Testament? I hear it often enough. "If the Pastor is preaching out of the Old Testament, we're not coming!" "The Old Testament is irrelevant since Jesus came!"

Statements like these break my heart. After all, the words of the Old Testament are no less inspired than the words of the New Testament. What Scripture do we think Paul was referring to when he told Timothy, "All Scripture is inspired by God and profitable for teaching, for reproof, for correction, for training in righteousness"?[141] The New Testament had not been compiled yet. So, he was referring to the text of The Old Testament.

J.I. Packer wrote, "Our aim in studying the Godhead must be to know God himself better. Our concern must be to enlarge our acquaintance, not simply with the doctrine of God's attributes, but with the living God whose attributes they are. As he is the subject of our study, and our helper in it, so he must himself be the end of it."[142]

---

[141] 2 Timothy 3:16, NASB.
[142] J.I. Packer, *Knowing God* (Downers Grove: Intervarsity Press, 1993), 23.

Perhaps you are not like me and things don't have to "line up." You can walk away from a puzzle with a missing piece and sleep like a baby. For you, you echo the line from the old hymn, "It is enough that Jesus died, and that He died for me."[143] On one hand, I applaud your faith. But, on the other hand, I can't help feeling that you are missing out on some of the wonder of God.

So, for those pilgrims on the path who need a reason to attempt to understand this glorious mystery, here's my list of why understanding Christ in the Old Testament is worth the journey.

- To understand how Jesus can be "the Lamb slain before the foundation of the world" and yet be born in a manger in the middle of human history.[144]

- To understand how the Bible can say "Jesus is the same yesterday, today and forever" and yet only live to be around 30 years of age.[145]

- To see that Jesus does, in fact, interact with human people at the point of their greatest need to show that He Himself is the solution to their every problem.

- To affirm the truth of the Bible's accuracy and inerrancy.

- To magnify and exalt the name of Jesus Christ as we are encouraged to do in God's Word.[146]

---

[143] "My Faith Has Found a Resting Place" in The Baptist Hymnal (Nashville: Convention Press, 1991), #412.
[144] Revelation 13:8
[145] Hebrews 13:8
[146] 2 Thessalonians 1:12

- To expand our view of the Glory of God in the person of Jesus Christ.

While these pre-incarnate appearances of Jesus Christ should expand our view of the Glory of God in the person of Christ, they are but mere shadows compared to an ultimate reality. These appearances do not compare to the actual incarnation when Christ took on human flesh and dwelt among men. The incarnation of Christ, Jesus being completely God and completely man at the same time, grants us the encouragement to live this Christian life in victory. The author of Hebrews wrote, "For we do not have a high priest who cannot sympathize with our weaknesses, but One who has been tempted in all things as we are, yet without sin."[147]

Nor do these pre-incarnate appearances compare to the magnificent reality of the indwelling of the Holy Spirit. In John 14, Jesus promised His disciples that after He went away, He would send to them another Helper, the Holy Spirit.

[16] I will ask the Father, and He will give you another Helper, that He may be with you forever; [17] that is the Spirit of truth, whom the world cannot receive, because it does not see Him or know Him, but you know Him because He abides with you and will be in you.

There are more passages that speak of The Holy Spirit dwelling within us than Christ dwelling within us. But, we must keep in mind that Jesus referred to The Holy Spirit, as "another" (of the same kind) Helper. So, in reality, it is Christ living in you, because The Holy Spirit is as much God as is Christ.

---

[147] Hebrews 4:15, NASB.

Look at John 14 for just a moment and let's notice something truly remarkable.

Jesus is gathered with His disciples for the last time. He will be arrested and tried later that night and crucified the next day. He is giving His disciples His farewell address. In verse 2, Jesus says, "In My Father's house are many dwelling places." Now, we understand that to mean that Jesus was referring to Heaven. You may have in your memory the KJV that says "mansions."

This is a Greek noun whose root word is the one that is translated for us as abide. So, this word means a place to abide or remain. The root word, *meno*, is used all throughout John 15 when Jesus pleas for believers to abide in Him.

Now, look down at verse 23, "Jesus answered and said to him, "If anyone loves Me, he will keep My word; and My Father will love him, and we will come to him, and make our **abode** with him."[148] This is the same Greek word as in v.3 translated dwelling place.

This is the ultimate fulfillment of the great promise of Immanuel, God with us.[149]

Listen to what Robert Boyd Munger writes,

"He was promising that just as He was going to Heaven to prepare a place for them and would one day welcome them there, so it would be possible for them to prepare a place for Him in their hearts now. He would come and make His home with them right here. This was beyond their comprehension. How could it be?

---

148 John 14:23, NASB.
149 Matthew 1:22-23, NASB.

Then came Pentecost. The spirit of the living Christ was given to the church, and they experienced what He had foretold. Now they understood. God did not dwell in Herod's temple in Jerusalem-nor in any temple made with hands! Now, through the miracle of the outpoured Spirit, God would dwell in human hearts. The body of the believer had become the temple of the living God and the human heart the home of Jesus Christ. **Thirty minutes after Pentecost the disciples knew more about Jesus than they had learned in the previous three years."**[150]

No longer do we have to look for a supernatural appearance of Christ to guide us, correct us or encourage us. We have the very presence of Christ dwelling within us. And that may be the greatest mystery of all.

---

[150] Robert Boyd Munger, My Heart Christ's Home (Downer's Grove: InterVarsity Press, 1992) p. 9.

One more thing...

Now that you've seen Christ from the very beginning of the Bible, all the way through the Old Testament, perhaps you can have a greater understanding of His arrival in Bethlehem.

One of the most amazing things about God is that He is so magnificent and complex but, at the same time, so simple that a child can believe in Him. After all, belief is the only requirement for having a personal relationship with God. So, I want to just lay out a few truths for you. These truths are not just random facts. They are truths about a person, a person who created you, loves you and wants you to spend eternity in the place He has created for you.

- **God has created us and the world around us. Thus, we are accountable to Him.**

"God created man in His own image, in the image of God He created him; male and female He created them." – Genesis 1:27

- **Every one of us is a sinner. We break God's laws.**

"for all have sinned and fall short of the glory of God,"- Romans 3:23

- **If we remain in our sin, without someone to rescue us, we will spend eternity separated from God.**

"For the wages of sin is death, but the free gift of God is eternal life in Christ Jesus our Lord." – Romans 6:23

- **God sent His Son, Jesus Christ, into the world to rescue us, die for our sins and make us right with God.**

"For God so loved the world, that He gave His only begotten Son, that whoever believes in Him shall not perish, but have eternal life." – John 3:16

- **When we put our trust in Jesus' sacrifice as the only way we can be right with God, He promises to give us eternal life.**

"if you confess with your mouth Jesus as Lord, and believe in your heart that God raised Him from the dead, you will be saved." – Romans 10:9

If you have never understood these truths, you have an opportunity to make the greatest decision you could ever make. By the death, burial and resurrection of Jesus Christ, God has offered you to know Him personally and spend eternal life in Heaven. Will you believe in Him? Will you put your trust in Jesus to save you from your sin?

The good news is that you don't have to get your life straightened out before you make this decision. God accepts you as you are. But, please understand, if you really do believe on Him and put your trust in Him, He will change you. He will make you into a different person. The Bible says in 2 Corinthians 5:17, *"Therefore if any man is in Christ, he is a new creature; the old things passed away; behold, new things have come."*

To make this life changing decision, it is as simple as asking. Right now, you can pray something like this…

God, I know that there have been many times that I have broken your law. I am a sinner. I understand that my sin needs forgiveness. I know that the only way for me to be forgiven is to believe that Jesus died so that I could live. So, now I put my trust in Jesus. I believe that He died for my sin. And now I want Him to make me new. I want Him to be my Lord and my Savior. In Jesus' name, Amen.

The words that you say are not as important as the attitude of your heart. If you put your trust in Jesus, He will save you, completely and forever. Following Jesus and getting to know Him will be the most fulfilling journey you could ever embark upon. He is worth trusting.

John M. Burris

Appendix One

Is Melchizedek a Christophany?

I t is the story of one of the strangest characters in the Bible, the priest/king Melchizedek.

Genesis 14:17-20

This is basically an aside in the midst of a story of a battle of nine kings and the capture of Abram's nephew, Lot. There are four Shemite kings: Amraphel of Shinar (also known as Hammurabi, King of Babylon or the Jews believe him to be Nimrod), Arioch of Ellasar (Assyria), Chedorlaomer of Elam (Iran) and Tidal of Goiim (Eastern Turkey-a coalition of barbaric peoples, the "*im*" on the end being a plural in the Hebrew language).

There are five Hamite kings: Bera of Sodom, Birsha of Gomorrah, Shinab of Admah, Shemeber of Zeboiim and the king of Bela. Some scholars believe the remains of Sodom and Gomorrah are somewhere beneath the Dead Sea.

In the midst of this battle, Abram's nephew, Lot, gets captured and this is what sends Abram into the picture. Apparently, Abram was a very important and wealthy tribal leader. So much so that he sent out his own militia (trained men born in his house Gen. 14:14).

Another indication of Abram's wealth and power is the fact that the King of Sodom goes out to meet him as if treading lightly toward the one who just routed the forces he had just been up against.

They met at the Valley of Shevah, or the King's Valley. This is to be identified with the region near Jerusalem where the Kidron valley meets the valley of Hinnom. Finally, we are ready to be introduced to the mysterious Melchizedek.

Here are the basic facts about Melchizedek:

- King of Salem (what would later be Jerusalem)- Psalm 76:2

- Priest of the Most High God (priests did not show up until 500 years later)

- Met with Abraham

- He blessed Abraham

- Abraham tithed the spoils of his conquest to Him.

- His name means king of righteousness

- By His being king of Salem, He was also king of peace (shalom-Hebrew for peace)

- He was without ancestry or descendants

- He had no beginning or end of life

- He was made like the Son of God

- He abides always as a priest

This is all that we know of Melchizedek. Who was this King/Priest? First, we have to draw a couple of conclusions:

1. All of the Bible is true, trustworthy and accurate.

2. God does nothing without purpose.

So, we have to conclude that there must be a good reason for God to include this obscure reference to a very unique person. Who is Melchizedek?

Understand that there are solid, trustworthy Biblical scholars who cannot answer that question with any degree of certainty.

One writer lists nine possibilities for an explanation of his identity. Some of those include; an angel, Shem or even Enoch. There is no biblical support for any of these other views.

Martin Luther seems to take the identity of Melchizedek to be Shem. He writes, "On the basis of the general conviction of the Hebrews it is assumed that this Melchizedek is Noah's son Shem. Even though not much depends on whether their conviction is right or wrong, I gladly agree with their opinion."[151] However, he could not be Shem because Hebrews 7:3 states that we do not know Melchizedek's genealogy. And, we do know Shem's genealogy.

There are a certain number of scholars who believe him to be a Christophany, or an appearance of the pre-incarnate Christ. This view has several implications.

In the following chart, you can see the direct correlations between the description of Melchizedek and Christ. It would not be out of bounds for Christ to make an appearance like this given His appearances in other passages and events prior to this one.

---

[151] Luther's Works Vol. 2, 381.

	Melchizedek Gen 14:18-20	**Christ**
Priest to Abraham	Abraham offered tithes to Melchizedek	Abraham saw Christ and rejoiced at his day. (John 8:54-59)
King and Priest in Jerusalem	Melchizedek was the King and Priest of Salem, (Jerusalem.)	Jesus will be both King and Priest of Jerusalem. Jesus was presented as King from birth to death. He prayed and interceded for the city. He will return as both King and Priest. Matthew 24:30, Matthew 27:37, Matthew 23:37-39,
Offers to Bread Abraham	Melchizedek offered bread, to Abraham after his victories of the	Jesus offered himself as the bread of life to Abraham's descendents. (John 6:33,53-58, Luke 22:19)
Offered Wine	Melchizedek offered wine to Abraham.	Jesus offered his blood as wine to Abraham's offspring (John 6:55, Luke 22:20-22)

Greater then Abraham	Melchizedek was greater then Abraham, because he received Abraham's offering for God.	Jesus was greater then Abraham (John 8:58) Aaron's priesthood was a picture of Messiah's greater priesthood.
Blessed Abraham	Melchizedek blessed Abraham	Abraham was blessed by Messiah (John 8:56)
King of Peace (Salem)	The name for Jerusalem is Peace (Salem). Melchizedek is King of Peace	One of the titles for Messiah is *Prince of Peace*. (Isaiah 9:6). Christ as King of Jerusalem fulfills the foreshadowing of Melchizedek. (Zechariah 14)
King of Righteousness	Melchizedek's name means "King of Righteousness"	Christ is the King of Righteousness
Priesthood	Not of the tribe of Levi	Of the Tribe of Judah (Genesis 49:10)
Duration	No Beginning and End	Eternal (Psalm 110;4)
Tithes	Received Tithes from Levi in the person of Abraham	Received tithes from Levi as the "Glory of the Lord" in His pre-incarnate state.
Tribe	Outside of Levi	Outside of Levi

While all of those are striking similarities, James Borland points to a few reasons why Melchizedek cannot be a Christophany.

1. When Christ did appear as a Christophany, he never came as a person in some way permanently tied to this earth.

2. If Melchizedek were Christ, then Christ could not be better than Melchizedek as the book of Hebrews implies. (Hebrews 7:22)

3. To say that Christ is a priest after the order of Melchizedek clearly distinguished the two from one another.[152]

The majority of Conservative scholarship believes him to be a literal king of a city named Salem in the territory of Canaan, what would later be Jerusalem. If he were only to appear in Genesis and not in Psalms and Hebrews, he may have disappeared into relative obscurity. The mention of him in those passages however, to those who see him as a literal king, make him a "type" of Christ.

Nelson's New Illustrated Bible Dictionary says the following about Melchizedek:

A king of Salem (Jerusalem) and priest of the Most High God (Gen. 14:18-20; Ps. 110:4; Heb. 5:6-11; 6:20-7:28). Melchizedek's appearance and disappearance in the Book of Genesis are somewhat mysterious. Melchizedek and Abraham first met after Abraham's defeat of Chedorlaomer and his three allies. Melchizedek presented bread and wine to Abraham and his weary men, demonstrating friendship and religious kinship. He bestowed a blessing on Abraham in the name of

---

[152] James Borland, *Christ in the Old Testament: Old Testament Appearances of Christ in Human Form* (Fern, Ross-shire: Christian Focus Publications, 2010), 146.

El Elyon ("God Most High") and praised God for giving Abraham a victory in battle (Gen. 14:18-20).

Abraham presented Melchizedek with a tithe (a tenth) of all the booty he had gathered. By this act Abraham indicated that he recognized Melchizedek as a fellow worshiper of the one true God as well as a priest who ranked higher spiritually than himself. Melchizedek's existence shows that there were people other than Abraham and his family who served the true God.

In Psalm 110, a messianic psalm written by David (Matt. 22:43), Melchizedek is seen as a type of Christ. This theme is repeated in the Book of Hebrews, where both Melchizedek and Christ are considered kings of righteousness and peace. By citing Melchizedek and his unique priesthood as a type, the writer shows that Christ's new priesthood is superior to the old Levitical order and the priesthood of Aaron (Heb. 7:1-10; Melchizedek, KJV). Attempts have been made to identify Melchizedek as... an angel, the Holy Spirit, Christ, and others. All are the products of speculation, not historical fact; and it is impossible to reconcile them with the theological argument of Hebrews. **Melchizedek was a real, historical king-priest who served as a type for the greater King-Priest who was to come, Jesus Christ.**[153]

One of the most important considerations in the typology is what is the order of Melchizedek? Psalm 110, which is one of the most often quoted psalms in the New Testament, declares, "Thou (Messiah) art a priest forever, according to the order of Melchizedek."[154]

---

[153] Nelson's New Illustrated Bible Dictionary, 819.
[154] Psalm 110:4, NASB

Christ was not said to be of the order of Aaron, or the order of Levi. What was Melchizedek's order? What did he do?

- He Blessed God (El Elyon- God Most High, a superlative)

- He brought forth bread and wine

Worship and sacrifice were Melchizedek's function or order to perform. That is the pattern that Christ is to follow. He would bring glory to the Father (blessing God) and would lay down His life as a sacrifice for sin, which He symbolized by bread and wine.

"In the Levitical economy, priest and sacrifice were inseparable; without priest, sacrifice could not be offered, and without sacrifice priest had no place. Both systems were to go on side by side until they finally met and were perfected in one centre. For be it remembered, that not only were the sacrifices typical, pointing to Him Who was to be "led as a lamb to the slaughter" (Isa. 53) - "the Lamb of God Which taketh away the sin of the world" - but the system of priesthood, too, was merely "serving unto the example and shadow of heavenly things ," pointing to Him Who was to come and be "a Priest for ever after the order of Melchizedek."[155]

Bread and wine, body and blood are always pointing toward the redemption offered in Christ. From the Chief baker and cupbearer in the story of Joseph in Genesis 40 (the chief baker is hanged by the way) to the manna in the wilderness and the pattern of blood in the sacrificial system. The order of Melchizedek was

---

[155] Baron, David (2013-12-17). Rays of Messiah's Glory (Kindle Locations 428-431). (Kindle Locations 426-428). Kindle Edition.

already pointing to a worship of the one true living God and the sacrifice that would make our redemption possible.

Appendix Two

The 39 Pre-incarnate Appearances of Christ in The Old Testament

1. Genesis 3:8

2. Genesis 5:22-24

3. Genesis 6:9

4. Genesis 11:5

5. Genesis 12:7

6. Genesis 15

7. Genesis 16:7-11

8. Genesis 17:1

9. Genesis 18:1

10. Genesis 21:17

11. Genesis 22:11-15

12. Genesis 26:2

13. Genesis 26:24

14. Genesis 28:13

15. Genesis 31:11

16. Genesis 32

17. Exodus 3

18.Exodus 4:24

19.Exodus 14:19

20.Exodus 17:6

21.Exodus 19:18-20

22.Exodus 24:9-11

23.Exodus 34:5

24.Numbers 11:25

25.Numbers 12:5-8

26.Numbers 22

27.Deut. 31:15

28.Joshua 5:13-15

29.Judges 2:1-4

30.Judges 6

31.Judges 13

32.1 Samuel 3:10-21

33.2 Samuel 24:16

34.1 Kings 19

35.2 Kings 1:3-15

36.2 Kings 19:35

37.2 Chronicles 7:12

38.Jeremiah 1:4-10

39.Daniel 3:23-25

Works Cited

Baker, Warren, Patrick, Warren, Zodhiates, Spiros. *The Complete Word Study Dictionary: Old Testament*. AMG Publishers, 1994.

Barclay, William. "Jesus as They Saw Him," in *The Book of Jesus* ed. Calvin Miller. New York: Simon and Schuster, 1996.

Barrett, Michael P.V. *Beginning at Moses: A Guide to Finding Christ in the Old Testament*. Greenville: Ambassador-Emerald International, 1999.

Bernis, Jonathan. "Finding Jesus in the Old Testament." www.charismamag.com

Borland, James. *Christ in the Old Testament: Old Testament Appearances of Christ in Human Form*. Fern, Ross-shire: Christian Focus Publications, 2010.

Buswell Jr., James Oliver. *A Systematic Theology of the Christian Religion*, 2 vols. Grand Rapids: Zondervan, 1962.

Cate, Robert L. *Old Testament Roots for New Testament Faith*. Nashville: Broadman Press, 1982.

Chaffey, Tim. "Theophanies in the Old Testament." https://answersingenesis.org/jesus-christ/incarnation/theophanies-in-the-old-testament/

Clowney, Edmund. *The Unfolding Mystery: Discovering Christ in the Old*
     Testament. Phillipsburg: P & R Publishing, 1988.

Crisp, Oliver. *Jonathan Edwards on God and Creation*. Oxford:
     Oxford
     University Press, 2012.

Grudem, Wayne. *Systematic Theology*. Grand Rapids: Zondervan,
     1994.

Heiser, Michael S. *The Unseen Realm: Recovering the Supernatural*
     Worldview of the Bible. Bellingham: Lexham Press, 2015.

Hershberger, Ervin N. *Seeing Christ in the Old Testament*.
     Harrisonburg: Vision Publishers, 2010.

Hodgkins, A.M. *Christ in All the Scriptures*. Forgotten Books, 2012.

Kaiser, Walter C. *The Messiah in the Old Testament*. Grand Rapids:
     Zondervan Publishing House, 1995.

Keil, C.F. and Delitzsch, F. *Commentary on the Old Testament, vols.*
     1--3. Peabody,
     Mass: Hendrickson Publishers, 2011.

Lewis, C.S. *Mere Christianity*. New York: MacMillan Co., 1953.

Luther, Martin. *Luther's Works vol. 2*. Concordia, 1960.

MacArthur, John. *The MacArthur New Testament Commentary: John*
     1-11.
     Chicago: Moody Press, 2006.

MacArthur, John. *The MacArthur Study Bible*. Nashville: Thomas
	Nelson
	Publishers, 2013.

MacArthur, John. "The Nature of the Incarnation, Part 2."
	www.gty.org ,

McGee, J. Vernon. *Thru the Bible Commentary vol. 3*. Nashville:
	Thomas Nelson Publishers, 1983.

Missler, Chuck. *Hidden Treasures in the Biblical Text*. Coeur
	d'Alene:
	Koinonia House. Kindle Edition.

Munger, Robert Boyd. *My Heart Christ's Home*. Downer's Grove:
	InterVarsity Press, 1992.

Murray, David. *Jesus on Every Page.* Nashville: Thomas Nelson
	Publishers,
	2013.

"My Faith Has Found a Resting Place" in The Baptist Hymnal.
	Nashville: Convention Press, 1991.

The NAS New Testament Greek Lexicon. "Charakter."
	http://www.biblestudytools.com/lexicons/greek/nas/charak
	ter.html

Packer, J.I. *Knowing God.* Downers Grove: Intervarsity Press, 1993.

Perman, Matt. "What is the Doctrine of The Trinity?"
	http://www.desiringgod.org/articles/what-is-the-doctrine-
	of-the-trinity

Pope, Kyle. "In the Beginning was the Word: A Study of the Logos Doctrine" www.ancientroadpublications.com

Poythress, Vern. *Theophany: A Biblical Theology of God's Appearing.* Wheaton: Crossway Books, 2018.

Read, W.E. "Christ The Logos-The Word of God." www.ministrymagazine.org

The Revell Bible Dictionary. "Jesus." New Jersey: Fleming H. Revell Company, 1990.

Sanders, J. Oswald. *The Incomparable Christ* Chicago: Moody Press, 1971.

Simpson, A.B. *The Christ in the Bible Commentary, Vol.2.* Camp Hill: Christian Publications, 1992.

Sproul, R.C. "Logos." www.ligonier.org.

Stewart, Don. "Who is The Angel of the Lord in the Old Testament." www.blueletterbible.org

Stone, J.D. "Jesus' Name." http://jdstone.org/cr/files/jesusname.html

Stowell, Joseph M. *Fan the Flame: Living Out Your First Love for Christ.* Chicago: Moody Press, 1986.

Vine, W.E., Unger, Merrill F.,White Jr. William, *Vine's Complete Expository Dictionary of Old and New Testament Words.* Nashville: Thomas Nelson Publishers, 1985.

Walvoord, John F. *Jesus Christ Our Lord.* Chicago: Moody Publishers, 1969.

Wiersbe, Warren. *Be Available (Judges): Accepting the Challenge to Confront the Enemy.* Colorado Springs: David C. Cook, 1994.

Youngblood, Ronald F., Bruce, F.F. *Nelson's New Illustrated Bible Dictionary.* Thomas Nelson, 1995.

Zodhiates, Spiros. *The Complete Word Study Dictionary: New Testament.* AMG Publishers, 1992.

http://www.bible-archaeology.info/abraham.htm

http://www.icr.org/home/resources/resources_tracts_whentheysa wthestar/

http://www.merriam-webster.com/dictionary/pre-incarnate

http://www.preceptaustin.org/angel_of_the_lord.htm

http://www.thebiblejourney.org/more-resources/talks/whats-in-a-word/

http://www.wineskins.org/2014/05/05/the-spirit-of-jesus/

CPSIA information can be obtained
at www.ICGtesting.com
Printed in the USA
LVHW040927301119
638508LV00003B/246